MAGIC: SCIENCE OF THE FUTURE

Joseph F. Goodavage

D0173837

A SIGNET BOOK from
NEW AMERICAN LIBRARY
TIMES MIRROR

Published by
THE NEW AMERICAN LIBRARY
OF CANADA LIMITED

*NAL books are also available at discounts in bulk quantity
for industrial or sales-promotional use. For details, write to
Premium Marketing Division, New American Library, Inc.,
1301 Avenue of the Americas, New York, New York 10019.*

ACKNOWLEDGMENTS:
   The following titles and articles first appeared in somewhat
different form in the publications listed below:
   "Magic: Science of the Future," *Analog*, December 1972.
Copyright © 1972 by the Condé Nast Publications, Inc.
All rights reserved.
   "The Incredible Hieronymus Machine," *Saga* Magazine,
September 1972. Copyright © 1972, Gambi Publications, Inc.
   "Contact!", *Saga* Magazine, January 1973, under the title
"Contact with Extraterrestrial Life." Copyright © 1973, Gambi
Publications, Inc.
   "The Curse of the Hope Diamond," *Fate* Magazine, September
1974. © September, 1974, Clark Publishing Co.
   "Suppression—in the Name of Science," *Saga*, Annual 1974,
under the title "Scientific Suppression in the Name of Science."
Copyright © 1974, Gambi Publications, Inc.

First Printing, July, 1976

1 2 3 4 5 6 7 8 9

Fraud, Fanaticism—or The Science of Our Future?

Radionics—a clever hoax devised by scientists, engineers, and a retired general, or an inexpensive means of wiping out insect blights?

Kirilian Photography—artistically doctored pictures, or the actual filming of the L-field, the vital energy aura necessary to all life?

Biofeedback—a placebo for the helpless and the hopeless, or a method of meditation which can teach you to control your body and conquer disease?

Biological Energy Waves—an unlocated, random pattern of noise, or an emergency message broadcast by beings from beyond our solar system?

At last the evidence is in, and the truth can no longer be denied! There are life-creating and preserving forces which cannot be explained away by disciples of the physical sciences. There have been too many successful and well-documented experiments which conclusively prove the validity of psionics for it to be laughed off as a madman's daydream. And this book fully explores this long-neglected subject, presenting the facts we have to date, and disclosing the wonderful possibilities and the hidden dangers which await us as we learn to control the most powerful force in the Universe.

SIGNET Books of Special Interest

Acknowledgments

To the many farsighted and dedicated friends and colleagues who have helped make this a most rewarding effort, I am deeply indebted. To George and Marjorie de la Warr for their unequaled contributions to this vast new dimension of scientific and philosophical inquiry. My thanks to T. Galen Hieronymus, General Henry Gross, Muriel Benjamin, Count Pino Turolla, Leonardo Corte, Dr. Harold S. Burr, Dr. Leonard J. Ravitz, Arthur M. Young, Frances Farrelly, Karlis Osis and Carl Betz for their generous contributions of time and help.

My special gratitude to Helen Robins for her unselfish and inspired assistance—to Edward W. Russell and Barbara Russell, and to my wife Evelyn for devotion and dedication above and beyond whatever the call of duty may have been.

Additional thanks to Ben Bova, Marty Singer and Mary Margaret Fuller, editors respectively of *Analog*, *Saga* and *Fate* magazines, for allowing me to use my titles and articles which first appeared in their periodicals as a basis for various parts of this book.

Joseph F. Goodavage

Whitefield, Maine

Contents

Introduction

The Brave New Science
of Psionics—

Poor Old God! ... we blame Him for that which we most regret and for which we despise ourselves most.

It seems unfair. But *are* human beings any more to blame than the Creator for our troubles? Do we actually have much to say about our fate as individuals or our destiny as a species? As far as it is now known, we have no choice about our sex or race—we have nothing to say about whether we're born or not born—or whether we come into this world (or any other) as human beings, chickens, or lizards.

Are people, therefore, to be held more accountable than, say, the ants or sparrows?

Human physiology provides some interesting clues. Except for breathing (a semivoluntary act), no function of your body is conscious or deliberate. "Something" keeps things working for you. Westerners are incredulous when a yogi demonstrates his control over his heartbeat, pulse, and rate of bleeding, but potentially we all share the same control.

Every few years each cell and molecule of your body is duplicated and replaced. *You* don't do it—not consciously, at any rate. Depending on your age, you've had a completely new brain from five to 25 times since you were born, yet you can often remember events and recognize facts that you haven't seen since childhood. The brain considers itself completely autonomous. Something on a higher order, however, controls its activity.

Through the plant and animal life you consume, your body and brain are composed of the elements of the land and sea. Physically, the human race is part of the Earth's crust. As a species, *we* didn't decide to be created. Our existence is

1

probably the only option we have in a deterministic Universe. It's the hand we've been dealt.

A Supreme pattern-making Energy or Power apparently caused life to appear from what scientists believe was the lifeless ball of primordial Earth. Evolution (which may be a reflection of this pattern-making Energy) influences matter by forcing it along the path of ever-increasing complexity. But Homo sapiens may not be its ultimate aim. We're now in the process of a physical kind of *non*evolution.

This is about all we know—or think we know—about what we are and where we're heading, or understanding the purpose of life. A mosquito, for example, is an extremely specialized organism, and so is a jellyfish. An enormous amount of creative thought and engineering know-how must have gone into the life concepts of the mosquito and the jellyfish. It seems inconceivable that there is not some "purpose" behind such effort.

To us, mosquitos seem to be utterly without redeeming value. If we could, we'd probably exterminate them once and for all, and to hell with consequences. We've repeatedly tried nearly everywhere on the planet, but the pesky critters are still buzzing around.

They appear to have a purpose which remains (to us) unfathomable. And if a jellyfish and mosquito serve some ecological function, what greater purpose is served by the entire ecology? Especially since we are part of it? Apparently the same Power or Energy responsible for microbes, whales, and trees is equally responsible for human destiny, so why are we so firmly convinced of our free will?

Maybe we're "programmed" to react this way. Either as a species or as part of a greater ecological sphere, Homo sapiens exists for an *ongoing* purpose, but as one eminent astronomer lamented, "There must be something better than Man in the Universe. There must be!"

Maybe not. Consciousness and intelligence, human creativity and love are integral to the Universe, so we're here for a reason. Our job is to discover what it is.

Since 1962, we've been studying the Universe from the threshold of a new age. The cosmos, rather than being merely a vast aggregate of gross material, begins to look more like a tantalizing nonphysical *principle*—a colossal, infinitely complex thought incorporating the mysteries of time, space, such invisible energies as gravity, and perhaps Creation itself. Each small mystery solved multiplies those that remain.

Whether we call the present nexus of history the Atomic Age, the Space Age, or the Age of Aquarius, we're now situated between two World Ages and caught up in a total revolution. We're developing new concepts involving time, space, gravity, and psychic and other forms of radiant energy, but for what purpose? In combination with scientific and technological advances, it is probably to prepare Homo sapiens for future interstellar voyages and contact with beings among civilizations from other star systems.

Our local Sun radiates in all wavelengths through the electromagnetic spectrum. Radio waves, light, and the other radiations from this EM spectrum flash around the planet at more than seven times a second. One of the major differences, for example, between visible and ultraviolet light is the wavelength or number of cycles per second at which these waves oscillate. It is this frequency of vibration that determines the difference, say, between gamma rays and radio waves. Differences in the frequency of visible light are detected by the human eye as color variations. All known electromagnetic radiation is essentially periodic changes of the electric and magnetic field of the Sun and Earth. They propagate in a vacuum at the same speed—approximately 186,200 miles per second. Their only difference is their *frequency*. If there are energies that vastly exceed the speed of light (at this point anything seems possible), we may need the help of computers or another form of intelligence to create devices capable of detecting them.

Thanks to Einstein and de Broglie, we're faced with the fantastic situation that energy and matter are both *interchangeable* and also one and *the same!* Radiation has the same properties as particles; material particles have the same properties as waves (of radiation). This creates the paradox that both matter and radiation (energy) have, at one and the same time, a dualistic *and* a similar nature!

This means that your body and brain and mine are composed of electromagnetic radiations "frozen" (by some mysterious attribute of time and/or gravity) into the physical bodies we've come to accept as our essential "self." If this seems as though human beings are actually solar radiation—temporarily solidified in a gravitational field—then two conclusions are possible: 1) any organism living for an extended period *outside* a gravitational field should exhibit the signs of physical debilitation such as was found among astronauts who'd been on long orbital flights, and 2) there should be a remarkable increase in psychic ability and telepathic communication in a null-gravity field. (Astronaut Edgar D. Mitchell gave the first demonstration of this undiscovered phenomenon by conducting a telepathic experiment with a psychic on Earth while returning from the Moon.)

Here are some interesting facts about radiant energy: light waves, for example, are *extre-e-emely* small. A hundred of them could be arranged in a row across the width of a single human hair. It takes *thousands* of ultraviolet waves to cross a distance that would require only a *few* waves of infrared (the two extremes of the visible spectrum). The frequency of electromagnetic radiation is *lower* on the infrared side of visible light and *higher* on the ultraviolet side.

When pioneer researchers discovered the existence of electromagnetic waves both longer and shorter than visible light, they figured that all they had to do then was to find out just how far these outer ranges reached. Today we recognize and use electromagnetic waves thousands of times shorter than light and others many miles in length.

There are probably wavelengths of thousands, perhaps millions, of miles. Some oscillate in a millionth of a nanosecond. There may also be waves that cycle only once every trillion seconds. To the pioneers in wave phenomena, facts like these surpassed their wildest expectations. Considering the enormous range of the electromagnetic spectrum, human senses are severely limited. Your eye can perceive only visible light—just a tiny segment of the high region of this spectrum.

There seem to be entirely different kinds of forces—waves of radiant energy *beyond* the EM spectrum. Gravity, for example, telepathy, and perhaps time itself may represent phenomena stretching on the farther side of human knowledge—*something entirely apart from anything ever measured.*

4

Perhaps it's more than a coincidence that the non-physical Mind is capable of conceiving and constructing instruments to measure waves that lie beyond the ability of physical senses to detect. It poses an interesting question: Why should Mind (which governs the brain's activity) have been able to predict the properties of electromagnetic waves whose existence had not yet been discovered?

The sheer immensity of the Milky Way Galaxy, the local galactic group, and the detectable radio Universe, in that order, pose some problems for scientists who believe that nothing can exceed the speed of light at 186,200 miles per second, "the highest possible velocity." Therefore, it would take a radio message (or a space ship) 100,000 years for a round trip to the middle of our own Galaxy.

The vastness of the cosmos is mind-boggling; if you visualize the Moon as a grain of sand, the Earth would be the size of an apple seed about two inches away. On this scale the Sun would be a large pumpkin almost a quarter-mile distant. The nearest stars would be smaller and larger pumpkins (some thousands of times bigger or smaller), each one more than a thousand miles apart. In Real Universe terms, the closest star is more than 2 thousand billion miles from the Earth—about four light years.

If we imagine that these stars are now suddenly reduced to the size of atoms, the resulting "molecule" (composed of roughly a hundred billion "atoms"—the stars of the Galaxy) would be 25 million miles in diameter.

Now, in your imagination, reduce this incredibly huge "molecule" (or incredibly *small* Galaxy) to the size of a bee and visualize a swarm of these galaxy-bees (each of which are thousands of miles apart) speeding away from each other in all directions at millions of miles an hour. They've been exploding away from each other like this for 13 thousand million years!

By turning the cosmic clock backward 13 billion years, scientists have estimated that the Universe began with a mighty explosion—a superstupendous flash of blinding white light. Astronomer Herbert Jastrow quoted Genesis: *"And God said, let there be light, and light was made. And God saw the light that it was good . . ."*

That light continues. We're all part of it. Not only do all the component cosmic bodies which are supposed to have resulted from that Big Bang (the swarms of Galaxies, stars, planets, and all living things) radiate on millions of different wavelengths, they seem to *be* radiation (in a kind of temporarily static or "frozen" condition).

Light from the Sun radiates at a constant velocity—186,200 mps. But the rate at which its energy oscillates varies from a cycle of one or two per second to 100 billion per second (and beyond) as we move past the gamma and secondary cosmic rays.

Some electromagnetic waves are *trillionths* of a second apart, some are a billionth, a millionth, or a thousandth of a second apart. They seem to gallop into infinity from both sides of the decimal point. Many waves range from thousands of seconds to *trillions* of seconds apart (a thousand seconds is about 16 minutes and a trillion is more than 27 years!). They can be measured or detected only indirectly through observation of their influence on the cycles of human history. In some highly advanced prehistoric civilization this may have triggered the discovery of what we call astrology because these waves coincide with solar activity and planets' positions.

Within two decades we've seen a total revolution in ethics and morals, lifestyle, art, religion, science, law—but particularly in the emerging self-image of human beings.

From the surviving records of the early days of natural philosophy, a few geniuses in each nation deduced the basic unity and harmony of the Universe. Invariably, they attributed this to some Divine Plan. Then along came regimented thinking that gradually organized itself into a series of mutually exclusive domains of expertise—the sciences. This was followed by the specialization which is currently fashionable. Since the Industrial Revolution, modern technology prompted scientists into reconnecting their various specialties.

They *had* to. Chemistry, when divorced from biology, just didn't lead anywhere or *mean* anything. Neither did physics when separated from astronomy and confined to the Earth. Later, as increased sophistication (microminiaturization of electronic components) introduced a kind of second (or perhaps third) industrial revolution which gave birth to machines capable of autonomous behavior (and now intelligence) the hyphenated sciences began to merge.

When biology merged with chemistry, there were new discoveries in genetics. Now astrophysics has combined with biochemistry to create the new field of exobiology—the search for possible life on other worlds. It's as though the power of human thought itself acts as a gravitational field, drawing accumulated knowledge to a center to create a super science.

Since 1962, for the first time in known history, Homo sapiens is seeing itself as a species which is—politically and sociologically—metamorphizing into something distinctly different.

We're already going about this by starting to rethink the laws of science (which do not now include all existing Truth). Scores of strange and fascinating machines have been patented which violate all the tenets of modern science. One of these is a device called the Hieronymus Machine (about which, more later). These psionic inventions—i.e., devices that focus human thought and emotion—were *independently* discovered and constructed by curious, talented people all over the world. They are capable of absolutely incredible feats. Here's how one of them works:

By placing an aerial photograph of an orchard, a farm or a forest in the slot of a quasi-electronic device and turning one of its dials, an operator can drive off (*or kill*) millions of voracious insects in the area covered by the photograph—but *only* if the negative isn't destroyed! It can do this at distances ranging from hundreds to thousands of miles. Such a device simply "cannot exist." According to scientists, it's impossible. But they *do* exist. Moreover, they work, have worked, and *continue* to work. Psionic devices operate according to as-yet-undiscovered laws of the Universe and the human mind. A spruce budworm infestation has been plaguing the entire state of Maine and most of southeastern Canada. In Maine alone, pesticides (proven to be ineffective) cost over $10½ million each year. Forest experts, entomologists, and other scientific authorities from both nations have been advised of these patented devices. Their reaction:

They will not look.

7

They refuse to investigate because most of their education consisted of learning what *had* already been done. That's one of the reasons no educational institution can honestly offer a course in "creative writing." *Creativity* is something you either have or you don't have. Nobody can *teach* it. Neither can scientific "genius" or "ingenuity" be given as a credit course. As a consequence, the products of most educational colleges and universities are acutely aware of what *can't* work. They "know" therefore, that by definition psionic devices are forever impossible; if they worked, they'd "violate" what the experts were taught and sincerely believe to be "the laws of science."

One of the chief difficulties in establishing the reality of psionics is the erroneous belief that if science doesn't know about it, it can't exist. Ergo, anything outside of science is automatically false. It does no good at all to offer an actual demonstration of the device. Orthodoxy *cannot* be made to look. Hence: "Hogwash! Nothing can eradicate insects from thousands of acres, especially from a distance of more than a hundred miles."

As long as it is socially anathematized, and absolutely denied, any individual backing the idea is subjected to powerful cultural pressure. Even commercial success won't convince them. It can be demonstrated that our culture does marshal powerful pressure against anyone backing such an idea, so how do you go about convincing a bigot that bigotry is wrong? How much evidence do you show, how much logical and persuasive argument do you mount, to overcome a deeply rooted prejudice?

You can't. It's virtually impossible—as those who try to enforce edicts that upset deeply entrenched emotional feelings have discovered to their chagrin. This almost qualifies as a natural law, yet psionics machines do work—*are* working. I've personally witnessed demonstrations of devices like the Hieronymus Machine—partly because I was curious and skeptical and partly because I had a powerful hunch that there *had* to be something valid about it.

A psionic machine seems to symbolize and utilize the power of Mind on a higher, more refined level. It's either the Mind

8

of the individual operator or the vast local reservoir into which we're all "plugged"—the Mass Consciousness.

Psionics is a level of science beyond atomic power and electricity, which are responsible for shaping our rather remarkable world. How different our lives would be if electricity had never been discovered or developed! What if Benjamin Franklin, Thomas Edison, Marconi, Steinmetz, and Tesla had not made their discoveries and inventions? For one thing, we'd have no energy problem, because there would be no industrial or domestic electrical machines or appliances. Moreover, there'd be no batteries, no internal combustion engines, no cars, buses, trucks, airplanes, or ocean liners, no air conditioning, no radio, television, telephone, news wire services, or computers.

Oh, sure ... we'd probably be using sophisticated gas mantles for illumination and traveling around in ultraplush Victorian-style steamships, steam-driven trucks, buses, trains, and even private cars. By 1981, after a century of intensive development, they would probably be pretty darned sophisticated, too. Human creativity being what it is, we'd probably have developed some kind of steam-powered aircraft. But after a century of nonelectrical progress, civilization as we know it today would be completely unrecognizable. We might even have reached the Moon (à la Jules Verne), but it would be a quaint, dead-end undertaking without the tremendous assistance of high-speed, computer-directed fail-safe systems and light-speed cybernetic decisions. All that hinges on electricity.

Science is the brain-child of that pattern-making entity, the human mind, which has always imposed "inner" concepts on the exterior environment. By virtue of his superior intellect, man has mapped out the heavens, explored the Earth, and classified nearly everything he has discovered. Most of this specialized knowledge is preserved, arranged, regimented, and classified into the manageable system we call *science*.

Yet all too often we tend to regard science (forgetting that it's our own invention) as something above and apart from man—a kind of mysterious "infallible force" that somehow gets things done—mostly in mysterious ways. An aborigine, suddenly exposed to any sufficiently advanced technology, is awed into submissively thinking of it as sheer magic!

We're not much better off than the aborigine. We congratulate science for conquering the ills that plagued us for most of our known history, yet millions are starving to death in agricultural nations while those in the industrially developed areas of the Earth are dying of liver, kidney, and heart failures, and diseases such as emphysema, cancer, and myriad genetic defects. Millions of babies no longer need perish of the disease against which medical science has developed vaccines: polio, diptheria, whooping cough (pertussis), lockjaw (tetanus), measles, rubella (German measles), mumps, and smallpox.

We *should* be healthier than at any time in history, but fewer babies are being vaccinated. Does this reflect some aspect of an Overriding System that controls human population? Can it be that when man threatens the existence of other families, genera, and species with his burgeoning numbers, he triggers a built-in population control mechanism similar to that which shuts down the body and permits a dying organism to expire without pain or grief?

Environmentalists usually invoke "the availability of food" to explain the relative rarity with which members of the animal kingdom outstrip the ability of the environment to sustain them. This seems to be a perfectly logical interpretation of the observed phenomena—on the surface. But so is the belief among certain tribes that the beating of tom-toms during an eclipse causes the Sun to reappear! You'd be wasting your breath trying to tell THOSE jokers that tom-toms haven't a bloody thing to do with the Sun. *They* won't listen either, but their error is at least understandable as medieval man's geocentrism before Galileo championed Copernicus' heliocentric theory. Although we've known better since the sixteenth century, we still say that "the Sun sets," "the Moon rises," and the like.

When a new discovery is finally accepted (by a generation that grew up becoming familiar with it), the shadow of doubt falls on a whole range of previously "accepted" theories. Case in point: Darwin's revolutionary concept of natural selection. There's nothing sacred about Darwin's theory except in the imaginations of certain Ph.D.s our institutions churn out with such maddening regularity. All too frequently they are educated beyond the capacity of their natural gifts.

The concept of the electrodynamic *Fields of Life* is more basic, far-reaching, and revolutionary than Darwin's theory. Our increased awareness of these fields tends to dramatize the narrowness of materialistic ignorance of the past. These invisible electrodynamic L-fields surround every organism as a kind of "aura." It is the "matrix" of life that shapes and controls your body and mine, and may be the "biological energy" connecting all life in the Universe. Moreover, L-fields may explain many of the questions posed by Darwin's "spin-off-from-the-apes" theory of the origin of mankind.

The discovery of L-fields shatters some pat theories about genetics and evolution, and provides the first rational, *demonstrable* explanation of the energy that *motivates* genetics. Even if they hadn't been discovered and detected with scientific instruments, the very concept of L-fields as the overriding biological control is a far better description of how the genes and chromosomes in egg and sperm are able to replace themselves, thus transferring genetic characteristics from one generation to the next. The fact that no mythological gods or demons are invoked by the proponents of field physics certainly ought to make the study of L-fields a completely acceptable and attractive scientific concept. It's more accurate and closer to the truth than the "blind, indeterministic chance" theory so dear to the hearts of the Darwinists.

An undiscovered ability of L-fields to control populations—possibly a "species specific" power—may control the combination of genetics among, say, ants and sharks so as to balance their numbers with all other populations, genera, and species of the terrestrial ecology. Such a theory is anti-evolution.

Nobel laureate S.E. Luria deplores the "creeping spiritualism" now threatening to invade the sacred domain of Big Science. "Many people, including some scientists," he says, "have refused to believe that a probablistic process like natural selection could have worked with such precision to bring about the almost uncanny fitness of plants and animals to their natural environments, as well as the marvels of the human mind. They have suggested the possible existence of biological laws other than those of physics and chemistry in order to explain the direction, speed, and apparent purposefulness of evolution ... Invoking unknown biological laws to explain the efficiency of natural selection is a return to vitalism, the theory that tried to explain the uniqueness of living organisms by postulating a 'vital force'! Such explanations explain nothing and, in the ultimate analysis, they can be traced to the metaphysical belief that each organism has a vital spirit or soul imposed upon it from outside."

One wonders whose *ultimate analysis* he's referring to. The learned doctor seems to imply that science has conclusively proven that biological organisms have no "vital spirit or soul." But the physical measurement of an L-field, an egg, a plant, or a human being, is a *hell* of a long way from that which orthodox geneticists describe as the "deplorable tendency" to invoke a nonphysical governing force to explain that which otherwise escapes their comprehension.

The L-field is inside *and* outside; it's above, below, and completely surrounding every chromosome and gene, every molecule, atom, and particle of your body as well as every other organism in, on or under the Earth—including the Earth itself, the solar system, the Galaxy—*and* the Universe.

The presently detectable segment of the L-field is probably a reflection or component of a supersentient force, a great conscious Awareness whose facets are time and timelessness, all energy, all matter, all we can know or imagine or dream—and all that is unimaginable. It is Everything and more—across, through, and beyond countless oceans of dimensions the human brain is not equipped to comprehend. It would, for example, be infinitely easier for a cat to master all the complexities of world government than for the physical brain to absorb the truth about the motivating Power of the Universe, the Source of Creation.

How do I know this? I can't "prove" it to the satisfaction of a hardheaded materialist.

But the *Mind*—ah, that's entirely different. *Mind* is "plugged in" to the Source.

Chapter One

—Threshold of a New Era?

"Human beings have a deep and desperate need to communicate with and relate to someone other than ourselves," said New York astronomer Richard Hoagland. "This is evident from our attempts at communication with other species right here on Earth—porpoises and whales—even plants."

Next to coming face to face with Almighty God, contact with intelligent alien beings may be the most shattering experience in human history. We may not even be *capable* of imagining the abyss that separates us—physically, intellectually, culturally, and emotionally—from such creatures. They might relate to us as we do to lower life forms such as fish, rodents, or dogs.

The open door to contact with such extraterrestrial beings could be a fantastic, quasi-electronic device called a "psionic" machine. There is reason to believe that when interspecies contact does occur—as it must if technological progress continues—it will probably be a beautiful, exhilarating, perhaps even ecstatic experience. At this stage of its development this is what the science of *psionics* seems to indicate.

If Erich Von Däniken's extraterrestrial visitation theories in his *Chariots of the Gods?* have any merit, contact with such beings may have inspired such profound psychic ecstasy among the ancients that they expressed their rapture as "worship." We now have scientific proof of the existence of extremely refined *fields* of emotion-triggering energy. These fields could be a kind of psychic equivalent to the chemical agents by which animals identify each other and detect fear or aggression through their sense of smell.

But more to the point, these forces could be a natural *psychic* energy associated with extraterrestrial Beings—the way

13

plants respond to human thoughts and emotions. Human beings may be equally responsive to the energy fields of extraordinarily complex nonhuman beings.

"Homo sapiens is undergoing a radical change," said ex-astronaut Edgar D. Mitchell. "Civilization is in a critical state and mankind is at an evolutionary crossroad."

Something is definitely happening to us as a species. According to U.N. Secretary-General Kurt Waldheim, "Mass human consciousness will be the decisive factor in determining the quality and condition of mankind's future life on this planet."

What *about* psionics? In 1956 the late science editor of *Analog* magazine, John W. Campbell, observed, "Psionics is the field of human achievement *beyond* science. He predicted that it would take 20 years before psionics machines were perfected and accepted. "But that can be and will be done," he said, "by 1976."

The requirement for scientific acceptance of psionics, he added, will be a viable theory explaining just how these quasi-electronic devices work and how they amplify, focus and project human thought and emotions. Voltage measurements of the "nonphysical" electrodynamic fields of humans can measure subjective states of consciousness such as hypnosis, deep meditation, affection, love, hatred and even more transcendental forms of energy. According to Wilhelm Reich of "orgone energy" fame, orgasm itself is essentially a psychic phenomenon.

The thrust of evolution is now toward examination and use of energies *beyond* the electromagnetic spectrum. Startling surprises lie ahead!

Astronomer Duncan Lunan of the University of Glasgow Observatory in Scotland recently discovered radio signals from an alien probe that entered lunar orbit 10,000 years before Alexander the Great conquered the known world. Unnatural delays in radio "echoes" from the mysterious device were found to contain a *message*. When the prestigious British Interplanetary Society processed these data by computer, a perfect image of the constellation Boötes emerged—*as it was seen from the solar system 13,000 years ago!*

In 1972, American physicist L. George Lawrence was using an advanced system of *psionics* instruments to detect long-range "signals" of flora in the Mojave Desert when his equipment detected signals from beyond the known electromagnetic spectrum. They gave every evidence of being faster than light and were coming from the direction of Ursa Major, a star system far off in the Galaxy.

Based on the accumulated evidence of similar data, we now have reason to believe: 1) advanced civilizations exist among most star systems, 2) interplanetary, even interstellar contact is the *rule* rather than a rarity, and 3) there is evidence that Homo sapiens may be *unconsciously* experiencing contact with them via extremely refined energies from space. Something seems to be influencing or guiding the human race. But toward what?

Homo sapiens is the most improbable, incomprehensible entity in the known Universe. No human ever lived who knew what he was, where he came from, where he was going—*or why*. But this picture is beginning to change. The study of psychic phenomena is at an all-time high; the mysteries of sex, intelligence, and race are being probed by genetic and biological engineers. We don't know whether intelligence is useful *or even necessary* to survival. Nevertheless, we're building machines with fantastically sophisticated computer brains. The Artificial Intelligence Groups at M.I.T., Stanford, and elsewhere have successfully built intelligence, consciousness, even self-awareness, into computers that are also autonomous!

Other scientists are feverishly working to learn about survival of physical death. The American Society for Psychical Research, for instance, receives federal and private grants to study such things as Mind Control, Transcendental Meditation, Biomagnetic Healing, Dowsing, astral projection—the whole panoply of psychic research—*and beyond*.

Psionics could not be explained until the recent discovery of the L-field, or Universal Field of Life (*the indestructible, nonphysical matrix that controls the physical form and function of all living things*). Scientists are learning about differences in energy potential between the brain and nonphysical Mind. They're building psychotronic generators and psionic *machines* that amplify human telepathic abilities and influence living things, mainly plants and insects, from great distances.

Nikola Tesla, the electronics genius who awed even Steinmetz and Edison with his brilliance, once observed, "When science begins the study of nonphysical phenomena, it will make more progress in one decade then in all the previous centuries of its existence."

It's happening right on schedule. Many psychics and clairvoyants can get a "reading" from a ring or wrist watch someone has worn. Others can bend metal at the molecular level with the power of thought, mentally manipulate light, and create pictures on a photographic emulsion with their minds. Still others use psionics devices to cure illness and disease—*or to kill*—at great distances.

Pizoelectric (i.e., electrically conductive) crystals—and diamonds—often emit strange radiations when stimulated. The "accursed" Hope Diamond, for instance, is the *only* blue-white stone that glows like a red-hot coal when bombarded by ultraviolet light. Those who have traced its history and pieced its story together believe there's "something substantial" to its alleged influence on the lives of people who have owned it.

Some suppressed inventions fairly boggle the mind, but they often help to illuminate the dark corners of the mass psyche. The Hieronymus Machine, for example, is a patented device that has been used to repel—and *kill*—millions of insects on hundreds of thousands of acres of farmland—merely from aerial *photographs* of the land!

A device patented in Great Britain called the Delawarr Camera is used to diagnose (and treat) human illness and disease—from great distances—according to certain unknown, recognized and completely baffling laws of the Universe. The Drown Machine is a patented American psionic machine. Its inventor, Ruth Drown, died shortly after being confined in a California prison while awaiting trial for medical fraud (after *successfully* treating hundreds of patients that doctors were unable to help).

These machines (I've personally collected the patents and seen many of them in operation) have circuit diagrams that in some strange way seem to detect, amplify, and direct human thought and emotion to accomplish specific objectives—*whatever thoughts are in the mind of the person who operates the machine!* This is a totally new concept of natural law; it makes Mind itself the controlling force of the L-field. As one of Albert Einstein's close collaborators (the Nobel Prize-winning physicist Pascal Jordan) reported, *"Gravity* has certain characteristics in common with the energy that transmits telepathic information ... both work at a distance and through obstacles."

Morris K. Jessup, American astronomer, physicist, archeologist, and psionics expert, was working on this theory before his mysterious and untimely death in 1959. He had devoted years to the investigation of great ancient stoneworks and engineering marvels of Egypt, Central and South America. No heavy trucks, earth-moving equipment, or crane ever built is capable of transporting 20,000-ton slabs of rock across hundreds of miles of rough terrain, lifting them high in the air, and grinding them back and forth, *in situ,* to a perfect fit.

The builders of Baalbeck did it thousands of years ago. "They were levitators," concluded Dr. Jessup, "who had mastered the secret of antigravity."

Did they know something that has since been forgotten? We're just beginning to rediscover the secrets of psionics, the apparent key to energies and forces reachable by certain qualities of the human brain and characteristics of the Mind. In the Trobriand Islands of the South Pacific, children are encouraged to participate unashamedly in open sexual play. To them, sex is the gods' gift to men and women for their happiness and pleasure. They believe that the gods arrange for babies to arrive in some mystical way on a large leaf and enter the woman's body through a tiny hole in the top of her head—but *only if she is married.* (Unmarried girls with babies are virtually nonexistent!) A suspicious anthropologist who observed them for three years tried to explain to them the connection between childbirth and sexual intercourse. The kindly people politely laughed at such an outrageous theory, but continued as they'd always done, with no precautions taken against pregnancy. The scientist finally concluded that the young women's emotional and mental conditioning gave them *automatic control over their feelings, bodies, and emotions*. They just didn't become pregnant when it was socially unacceptable to do so!

The same principle was introduced by a radiation therapist at Travis Air Base Hospital in California. The young doctor, whose work is more fully detailed in Chapter 5, trained terminally ill cancer patients to cure themselves through *meditation*, during which they visualized their body mechanisms at work healing and curing their disease. Result: 75 percent of his terminally ill patients experienced total remission! And as Ruth Drown taught, "Whatever we can do within our own bodies can also be done to help others with these electronic machines—even at a distance."

In the late 1940s three astonished Commerce Department officials wrestled with their consciences over a device that couldn't possibly work, yet did. It took three years before they granted U.S. Patent No. 2,482,773 to one T. Galen Hieronymus, thus unleashing a wave of controversy and fear as strong as some emotional reactions to real or imagined demon possession. But the Hieronymus Machine is not a fiction. The inventor tried to calm the rising tide of terror among those who knew enough to appreciate the potential of the thing he'd built:

"There's an energy radiating from, or a force field surrounding each isotope or element of material matter in the Universe. When two or more elements are joined together into a molecule of that matter, that molecule radiates an energy that is peculiar to that compound. (*Columbia University scientists recently made the same discovery*.)

"Instruments have been invented and patented that can 'tune in' to these radiations. By careful and skilled use of Eloptic (i.e., electrical and optical) Energy with such instruments, it is possible to analyze almost anything in the material world and to discover the constituent components . . . . .

"The energy can be refracted through a prism and conducted along light rays. It can be conducted along copper wires, through electronic condensors and capacitors, and manipulated like electricity.

"The energy from *a human being* can be conducted along

18

light rays and implanted on a light sensitive film, and again onto a *print* made from that film. The print can be moved to any distance away from the person, changing from moment to moment as the person changes. It was this principle that we used in order to follow the Apollo astronauts (8 and 11 through 17) into space and test them as they changed due to gravity and to other influences throughout the lunar flights."

Even though it seemed to make sense—almost, the damned thing posed a major paradox: the principles on which Hieronymus *said* it operated are beyond anything known to science. Yet hundreds of independent experiments have confirmed his claims by duplicating everything he said his device could do. Within the last year, Bell Laboratories and other electronics companies have been negotiating for the rights to his patent. In the Soviet Union scientists have employed psionics devices with Kirlian photography (to capture in color and stop or time-lapse motion picture photography the dazzling electrodynamic patterns from living organisms) to obtain almost mind-boggling results.

The Soviet Academy of Sciences seems to be far ahead in these studies. It has been called "radionics" as well as psionics, radiesthesia, and even bionics. Nikola Tesla detected the energy in living organisms, in magnets, crystals, and even blood samples. The "Father of Radionics," Dr. Henry Abrams, called this force Mitogenic radiation, Mesmer called it Animal Magnetism, Baron von Reichenbach said it was the Odic Force, Wilhelm Reich termed it Orgone Energy, Hieronymus says it's Eloptic Radiation.

They were all, of course, referring to the same force, about which a totally new scientific concept of the Universe is now being formulated among accepted and respected institutions such as Yale, Duke, the University of Pennsylvania and other centers of higher learning.

A search of foreign patent offices during the past seven years has netted variations on the Hieronymus Machine in England, Germany, Australia, Canada, and throughout Western Europe. Each one of them has its own astonishing tale—and *each was discovered independently!*

A psionic device called U.K.A.C.O. was developed by the Homeotronic Research Foundation in Harrisburg, Pennsylvania. The founder was Brig. Gen. Henry R. Gross (ret.), former state director of Selective Service in Harrisburg. He stimulated and increased the growth and yield of hundreds of thousands of acres of farmland throughout Pennsylvania, in New Jersey, Texas, California, and Arizona. (Now a happily retired almost 90-year-old multimillionaire, Gross has donated all his machines and life's work to Mankind Research Unlimited, Inc., in Washington, D.C. This heavily funded private organization is planning a total public release of their findings within three years.) General Gross and his colleagues successfully repelled billions of insect pests and killed billions more—simply by placing *photographs* of the blighted farmland in compartments of their psionic devices and turning certain dials.

An organization called the Round Table Foundation was established in Camden, Maine by the world-famous neurologist, Dr. Andrija Puharich to build and test every known model (and adaptation) of psionic device. Skilled technical and professional help streamed in from all over the U.S. and abroad. Energy from *beyond* the known electromagnetic spectrum was repeatedly amplified and directed with complete precision anywhere on Earth—and in two instances to the Moon and beyond.

Drs. Harold S. Burr and Leonard Ravitz devoted 40 years to the study of the L-field at the Yale University School of Medicine (and at Duke, and the University of Pennsylvania Schools of Medicine).

"These Fields of Life are now recognized as the basic blueprints of all life. Everything on Earth—from men to mice, from seeds to trees—are moulded and controlled by them—and are controllable, in turn, by the human mind . . ."

The discovery of the existence and function of L-fields has broadened to include the new science of exobiology. "It has enormous significance for all of us," said Dr. Burr. "Life is no accident, after all. In fact the Universe and all life forms everywhere belong to a profoundly meaningful and beautifully ordered system . . ."

If he's right, it must logically follow that the same laws apply equally to advanced civilizations in the region of Arcturus, or to intelligent creatures living on planets circling Alpha Centauri.

"The Earth is the cradle of mankind," said Soviet physiologist Leonid L. Vasiliev, "but no one remains in the cradle forever."

From a purely technological viewpoint, the third industrial revolution (mainly ultramicrominiaturization of electronics) indicates that the planets, stars, and even distant Galaxies figure in human destiny. But there's more—much, much more. The refined energies briefly outlined here indicate forces that exceed light speed by *multiples* of its own velocity! It relates these forces to gravity, telepathy, the Universal Field of Life, and energies beyond the L-field that are yet to be discovered.

The great Jesuit anthropologist and paleontologist, Pierre Teilhard de Chardin, predicted that Mass Human Consciousness would eventually evolve to surround the Earth with a kind of psychic shield he called the *"Noosphere."* It may be no coincidence that only the planets of the solar system which have atmospheres seem to be capable of supporting life. Perhaps a precondition for life and a balanced ecology are certain "rates" of gravity interwoven with a "charge" from the great reservoir of Universal Mind responsible for the L-field—or of which the L-field is a part.

Mass human awareness of these discoveries is accelerating rapidly; it's striking a wider and broader chord of response and is leading to the inescapable conclusion that it all "means something." Nikola Tesla's prediction appears to be borne out by the current wave of psionic research and development— *scientific investigation of nonphysical phenomena will be the greatest adventure in recorded history*.

All great religions have had one philosophy in common: that mankind must learn to master its baser nature and develop its far greater and more highly refined potential. Incredible as it once seemed to early twentieth-century materialists, it all seems to be coming together at some neutral midpoint between science, technology, and religion. My personal hunch is that we will make the breakthrough—but probably not without some rather exotic assistance.

The reward for these efforts could be anything between

some unbelievably exotic interspecies life-energy symbiosis from other worlds to a brilliantly intense awareness of an awesome Entity that lies beyond our wildest physical imaginations.

As a species, we've *already* left our cradle. It's conceivable that we may also be reaching the end of our adolescence. The potential to beat our swords into plowshares has always been within us. Once these psionic discoveries are widely recognized, an idea greater than anything in known history will give us the necessary motivation—on a global scale—to make the decision our ancestors may have failed to make several thousand years ago—to accept control of and responsibility for the continuation of our existence as a species.

Chapter Two

Suppression—
in the Name of Science

Charles Fort, the greatest of all science-baiters, enjoyed deflating the self-esteem of stuffed-shirt scientists. "The so-called great triumphs of science," he once remarked, "are always achieved against the savage resistance of scientists." He was right, too. Fort's inexhaustible source of data from which he collected examples of scientific arrogance, blundering, and vindictiveness, was the history of science itself. As another philosopher said, "The nature of man lies in his history." So it is with science.

Discoveries currently being suppressed include: 1) remedies for cancer, 2) cures for arthritis and paralysis, 3) radionic devices and psionic machines capable of miracles of diagnosis and treatment, 4) dowsing devices to detect water, oil, gold, uranium, coal, and so forth, 5) the discovery of rudimentary life within the solar system, 6) new discoveries about extrasensory perception, and 7) the monumental works of Immanuel Velikovsky and other potentially great names whose discoveries conflict with the *opinions* held by orthodox scientists.

Science doesn't solve problems in a straightforward manner; instead it does more to cloud facts, hide its mistakes, and create a repressive intellectual atmosphere than did the Church of the Middle Ages. The role of science in America's space program is a prime example. Rockets are okay for short hauls, but to reach the stars we *must* have an engine capable of modifying gravity. There is such an engine. It's called the Dean Drive, an odd-looking contraption consisting of counterrotating eccentric masses that converts rotary momentum to vertical lift.

The Dean Drive qualifies as a discovery/invention that has

been suppressed due to *ignorance* of the laws of gravity. The statement of Newton's Third Law, "For every action there is an opposite and equal reaction," often creates the impression that the mystery of gravity has been solved.

It hasn't.

To date, *nobody* knows the exact nature of gravity, how it is generated, or what makes it work. We'll never be able to explore interstellar space without somehow mastering it. This means we're going to have to go back and restudy Newton—and *then* some! Back to the earliest days of physics—back to Galileo and before him. For a clearer understanding of gravity and inertia we may have to begin all over again (with rudimentary mechanistic devices such as weights, centrifugal gadgets, torsion balances, and so on).

Even the planets of "our" solar system will never be explored by rocket power alone. As for the stars—forget it. With rockets it would be about as difficult as it is to sail all the way to Pluto—*by balloon!*

Consciously or not, Big Science is *suppressing* a principle necessary to build a true space drive, because there's little recognition of the need for it. The Dean Drive transforms rotary motion into lifting force. The widespread scientific belief that Newton's Third Law is the final word on gravity is keeping scientists from even looking at a demonstration of the Dean Drive because they already "know" its success is "impossible." This kind of inertia is what drives true discoverers mad with frustration.

Built by inventor Norman Dean of Washington, D.C., the prototype of the demonstration model is a device with counterrotating eccentric masses that generate a powerful *nonreactive* force. When the machine is placed on a scale and turned on, some of the weight goes—well, *somewhere.* This "violates" the Law of Conservation of Momentum, and today's scientists are in pretty much the same position as the members of the Holy Inquisition in Galileo's day. They "knew" that the Sun was "an absolutely perfect body" without flaws or blemishes. So when Galileo told them to *look* at the sunspots through his telescope, not only did they refuse, but he was charged with heresy for his efforts. Big Science is very much like the Church of the Middle Ages.

More important—it has the same characteristic prestige and even more power. Contrary to widespread, popular belief, all the great scientific and medical advances credited to "scientific" progress are not *BECAUSE* of science, but *IN SPITE* of it! Modern science does *NOT* encourage individuality or the kind of bold, independent thinking that leads to new inventions and discoveries. It *suppresses* them!

Paradoxically, while squelching some of the most beneficial-to-mankind advances, Big Science supports the chilling, Orwellian practice of brain surgery on social and political misfits—a practice even the Soviet Union has banned. But not here.

In these "enlightened times" science intellectually suffocates anyone who won't play the game their way. Supported by a kind of academic and industrial Mafia, Big Science has the money and power to enforce its edicts. Hovering octopus-like in the background is the military and industrial combine about which General Eisenhower repeatedly warned. The most influential political figures can't oppose such power and survive. In order to keep from spinning his wheels in this intellectual maze, the inexperienced young scientist is under incredible pressure "to publish." Relevance to anything going on in the "outside world" is negligible, insignificant, or coincidental. If he wants to succeed, he'd better damn soon learn to churn out at least one "important research paper" a year—the equivalent of a 300-page book. The name of the game is bigger and better financial grants from government and big foundations, which amounts to a pointless charade of ego and power.

Case in point: B. F. Skinner, one of Harvard's outstanding materialistic humanists. Paradoxically, he held a preconceived and misanthropomorphic bias (he seems to regard humanity as nearly worthless—almost a total loss). Yet he was awarded a 10-year *continuing* federal grant in the staggering sum of $283,000 for his "psychological research"—*even though his views were well-known!* With this king's ransom, he wrote the best-selling book, *Beyond Freedom and Dignity*, in which the good professor advocated massive human behavior control—via "positive reinforcement." Skinner believes that Man is essentially an animal, and a rather dangerous one

25

at that. Why? Because Man holds "delusions of his own grandeur" . . . dignity, freedom, and integrity? They hold no more significance for a human being than for a fish, frog, or snail, in Skinner's mind. He may be right about freedom, but what about human dignity and integrity?

The quarter-million-PLUS dollars was handed over by the National Institute of Mental Health. N.I.M.H., incidentally, publishes enough books, pamphlets, and journals to make any large publisher envious.

As if to emphasize Big Science's arrogance, avarice, and ignorance, a federal grant of $3 million dollars was made to former President Nixon's internist, Dr. Arnold Hutschnecker, who dreamed up a plan to administer *"a predictive psychological test for the criminal potential of all six to eight year old children in the nation."* Under Hutschnecker's proposed plan, the kids who *flunked* these tests are "to be sent to rehabilitation centers in a romantic setting out West." *(His own words!)*

Science's influence in the space program alone should stand as a massive indictment of scientific suppression. An excellent job of public relations has given Big Science undeserved credit as the originator of America's achievements in space. However, from Mercury to Gemini to Apollo to Skylab the fact is that our space feats were *technological, NOT* scientific triumphs. Theoretical scientists didn't build the rockets and establish the communications, power, and life-support systems, it was the "nuts and bolts" engineers.

Forrest Ray Moulton, the great astronomer and physicist of a few decades ago, ridiculed man's ancient dream of sending a vessel to the Moon as "a childish fantasy . . . anybody who knows anything at all about celestial mechanics knows that space travel and rocket ships are and always will be impossibilities. We will never be able to send a space ship to another planet, let alone *a man!*"

It sounds vaguely familiar. So does this:

Not long ago, the collective opinion of all sciencedom held that the speed of sound was "an insuperable barrier . . . nothing can ever exceed the speed of sound." But one physicist qualified the statement with two words: *"and survive."* These men forgot that their equally unimaginative predecessors said

the same thing about horseless carriages. "Even if such velocities were possible," griped one turn-of-the-century sourpuss,
"no human being could tolerate speeds in excess of 25 miles
an hour!"

Today's pundits have chosen *light* as the "final, ultimate,
impossible-to-surpass barrier in the Universe." *Sure* it is—IF
you're using chemically powered rockets. It's just as legitimate to claim that it's impossible to send instruments to
Mars—*by balloon*. Today's Saturn V boosters are naturally
out of the question as far as voyages to the planets and stars
are concerned. We're not going to put men on Venus or Mars
using fuel-gulping, 36-story monster rockets.

Rockets like the Centaur, Atlas, and Saturn, powered by
enormous quantities of expensive liquid oxygen and other
chemicals, are nearly totally cannibalistic. All but a small
fraction of the fuel they carry is consumed *just to boost the
rocket's final stage into orbit!* The last fraction of fuel is spar-
ingly rationed for use *later* in the flight. They carry *thousands*
of times more fuel than actual payload. To maintain even a
modest lunar colony of less than a hundred men and women
would, at this rate, quickly bankrupt all the world's wealthiest
nations.

"What we need," said one General Dynamics scientist, "is
a less costly, more powerful space drive." We *need* it, but do
the corporate scientists *want* it? Apparently not, because the
beginning of such an engine *already exists!* It's called the
Dean Drive and operates on a little-known principle of vibration that partially neutralizes the tug of gravity. In terms of
fuel consumption alone, this ought to make an immediate, intensive study of the Dead Drive so irresistible that space
scientists would give it top priority.

*Yet this revolutionary invention has been effectively
suppressed!* Scientists who actually *saw* it in operation devoted more time theorizing on why it "couldn't work" than in
giving it a fair study and critical tests. The bone of conten-
tion, according to some of the experts is that no existing theory can explain *why* it works. Incredible as it seems, this is
actually the excuse the scientific hierarchy gives for ignoring
it. *The fact that it does work is regarded as inconsequential*
because "it conflicts with the mathematical models which say

it can't." This is maddening to the inventor, who gets to feel like Alice in Wonderland where they keep changing all the rules to suit some totally obscure, illogical, or reactionary theory. To protest too loudly could mean something analogous to "Off with his head!"

The scientific Mafia flatly refuses to look—and *nobody* can make them. On every test it has been given, the rudimentary Dean Drive demonstrated its uncanny ability to dissipate the pull of gravity.

You don't have to be a genius to appreciate what such a simple mechanical contrivance would mean if a proportionately larger and more sophisticated version were to be installed in a large space ship. A group of British technicians did just that and improved the Dean Drive's performance by converting more of its mechanical action into energy.

The new version of this engine, as described in the British scientific and technical publication *Uranus,* is 10 feet tall and gives every indication of being the answer to a spaceman's dream. (Its developers call it the "Vortella.") At first they enthusiastically presented it to one scientific group after another. They repeatedly showed how the Vortella could lift and accelerate great masses to near-light speeds in less time and at less cost than a photon or ion drive. The more they demonstrated it, however, the more it was ignored, ridiculed, and rejected.

"We might have expected it," engineer Patrick Ryan wryly commented. "This is a real scientific breakthrough, but the pundits give it a cold reception. They refuse to admit that it is their own abysmal ignorance of basic scientific principles which prevented them from inventing it themselves."

Without support, the small group of engineers and technicians who developed and promoted it at their own expense ran out of money. If past performance is any criterion, chances are that the first Terran starship to visit another solar system will be an advanced version of the Vortella and/or the Dean Drive. That may take another quarter of a century, but we *could* have it now.

Ryan and his colleagues faced the same attitude as that exhibited by the know-it-all superintendent of the United States Patent Office back in the 1890s when he made the gratuitous and astonishing statement that "Everything that *can* be invented *has* been invented. There won't be anything from now on that isn't a simple deviation from what we now have. There's just nothing more that can be learned or invented." His solution? . . . that the government close down the Patent Office, disband its personnel, and dissolve its operations!

Like most laymen of the time, he was absolutely sincere in his belief that the *balloon* was the ultimate form of air travel. The didactic theorists of today, in spite of the mysteries posed by tachyon particles, quasars, and pulsars, and black-holes in space, stubbornly insist that nothing will ever equal the speed of light. They're utterly sincere, but they lack the vision to perceive that today's giant rockets are in actuality the "gas bag balloons" of space travel. For a rough approximation of the differences that will exist between today's cumbersome, wasteful rockets and tomorrow's infinitely more swift Leviathans of the stars, just compare the capacity and speed of a hot air balloon with that of a 747 jetliner. "Around the Galaxy in 80 Years" won't be far from the truth.

British science writer and novelist C. P. Snow pointed out that science "is a culture of its own, separated from the rest of society by a psychological gulf nearly impossible to overcome." Nowhere is this more apparent than in specialized medicine. Doctors who exclusively diagnose and treat some remote portion of the human anatomy often enjoy incomes well into the six-figure bracket. A specialist in cancer of the prostate, for example, is likely to scream "quack" if anyone dares to suggest that a relatively simple treatment might cure his patient.

Instances of scientific suppression of a new medical discoveries within the past 40 years would fill a couple of good-sized volumes. When Fred Wortmann, an 88-year-old maverick from Albany, Georgia, developed a large intestinal cancer, doctors assured him it wasn't hereditary, and insisted he needed immediate, drastic surgery.

"If it isn't hereditary," the spry old gent wondered, "how come three people in my family had it?"

The doctors shook their heads and chalked him up as another old crackpot teetering on the brink of a lingering death, useful only to medical students as a cadaver to slice up. But

Wortmann wasn't having any. "In all my experience," he said, "I've never seen *one* genuine internal cancer cured by surgery or any other orthodox treatment."

He searched for an *un*orthodox treatment and learned that 50 years previously some medical men from Pretoria, South Africa, had brought something called the Grape Cure to the United States. Although they had a good record of successful treatments, they were bitterly opposed as "quacks" by the medical fraternity.

"I revived the Grape Cure," Wortmann *(suddenly hale and hearty)* reported on his 90th birthday, "and shortened it from twelve hours to a six-hour-a-day diet. Instead of fresh grapes as in the original formula, I used unsweetened Concord grape *juice* as the best choice because it was available on a year-round basis at the grocery store.

"In more than 100 cases of victims of terminal cancer who had only weeks to live, all but two people got well by going on this half-day diet. Those two were so far gone with cancer of the liver that *nothing* could have saved them.

"Usually after six weeks on the diet, the most virulent cancer disappears. Bone and prostate cancer require about eight weeks, and the cost is roughly $16 to get well, as compared to the cost of dying to a lingering cancer patient of about $7,000. [That was in the preinflation 1960s.]

"The truth is so fantastic, nobody believes it. So I just tell anyone suffering from the disease to get in touch with me. I charge them *nothing* for telling them how easily they can recover."

Wortmann was vilified, threatened, and damned for his humanitarian efforts. But in the years prior to his death *(of a heart attack,* incidentally), he spread the word to thousands of cancer patients. His only reward: a filing cabinet filled with letters of gratitude from ex-cancer sufferers.

Vested interests with enormous political influence have successfully silenced one of the most amazing scientific and medical breakthroughs of all time. *Radiesthesia,* the diagnosis of illness by a doctor even though the patient is miles away— and *radionics,* the *treatment* of illness and disease (from a distance) was discovered by Baron von Reichenbach in the nineteenth century and independently *rediscovered* (over and over) during the next 85 years—all to no avail.

Ruth Drown, an enormously successful practitioner of radionics and manufacturer of the Drown Machine, was hounded by the courts for years. She died in a California prison while awaiting trail for treating and curing people with her device. George de la Warr, who developed a radionic diagnostic instrument (the Delawarr camera) at Oxford, England, was labeled a "quack" by medical men who had never seen his device, but who nevertheless "knew" you can't diagnose or treat a human illness by placing a blood sample of the patient into an electronic instrument and turning a few dials while the patient is at home or at work. De la Warr died almost broke after devoting his life and fortune to the development of radionics. Others have actually been driven out of the U.S. by the Food and Drug Administration and other government agencies. Nearly every one of these successful treatments were rejected as "inconsequential" or "practicing medicine without a license."

This is odd, because if it is "impossible" to treat an illness at a distance, then *nothing* is being "done" to the patient; therefore no "medicine" is being "practiced." *In effect,* a patient with a terminal illness is prevented *by law* from seeking unorthodox treatment for his condition. Yet orthodox medicine (if questioned closely) *admits* that it cannot save the life of a patient it has labeled "terminal."

During the 1940s and 1950s, independent investigators and inventors like T. Galen Hieronymus built and patented several very effective radionic machines. Repeated attempts to get a fair hearing from every conceivable official, bureau, or private foundation were either rejected or completely ignored—in *every* case—without cause or study. Interest in radionics is now being revived after a 14-year enforced hibernation.

According to the hierarchy of meteorologists at the United States Weather Bureau, only THEY are qualified to make forecasts. Those who need an accurate forecast most will swear that the USWB is almost *never* right, and on "long-range" forecasting (i.e., two to three days in advance) they're nearly always wrong! Despite billions of dollars poured into weather "research" (thousands of expensive meteorological balloons, intricate instruments, scores of aircraft, rockets, and weather satellites, not to mention 15,000 ground observers), the American Meteorological Society dazzles us ordinary mortals with filmflam and gobbledegook that *sounds* plausible but that's all. Undaunted, the experts at the USWB and the AMS are NOW making weather predictions for *Venus, Mars,* and *Jupiter* (whose effects seem to be *responsible* for terrestrial weather and earthquakes)!

Meteorologists have consistently rejected the idea that weather patterns could be caused through these extraterrestrial agents. They hold pioneer weatherman Irving P. Krick up to ridicule for such beliefs. But those who are interested in results instead of theory recognize this private, unorthodox climatologist as one of the world's foremost weather experts. His worldwide clientele includes foreign governments, covers all kinds of climate, in all kinds of terrain—with target areas ranging from golf courses and two-by-five-mile ski resorts to multimillion-acre range and farmland.

The map on the wall of Krick's Palm Springs headquarters reveals some of his operations: orchard owners in Georgia and Colorado, wheat farmers in Nebraska and Washington, sugar growers in Louisiana, cattle ranchers in Texas and New Mexico, and soybean farmers in Minnesota—some of which have been with him for 25 or 30 years.

Obviously, Krick is giving the kind of service the USWB can't provide. Like other researchers who have independently discovered the basic cause of weather, he once freely offered his discovery to the meteorological scientists—only to be ridiculed at each hearing. Yet his consistent accuracy over decades of private practice has made monkeys out of his detractors, which simply deepened their hatred of him.

Irving Krick studied worldwide weather patterns for many years. By the late 1930s he established to his satisfaction that weather behaved with form and rhythm. Up to this point, he had the attention of a few conventional meteorologists. "We came to think of the Earth's atmosphere as a kind of elastic envelope in which various *extraterrestrial* forces set up traveling wave forms which affect barometric patterns discernible at ground level.

As General Dwight D. Eisenhower's best-known meteorologist during the Second World War, Krick headed the team that successfully chose June 6, 1944 as the best date, weatherwise, for the D-Day invasion. "All weather is controlled by lunar and solar atmospheric tides and other extraterrestrial forces," he maintains.

"Inconclusive and indefinite," scoffed Francis W. Reichelderfer, who was then chief of the Weather Bureau. His agents actually followed Krick wherever he went to forecast or modify rain patterns (he was the first man to successfully control rainfall by cloud-seeding with silver iodide). They told the drought-suffering farmers that Krick was an "unscientific quack."

"Well," Krick retorted, "that's better than being a *scientific* one; at least we get things done. The Weather Bureau is still in the Dark Ages."

Twenty-five years after Krick and Vincent Schaefer learned *how* to cause rainfall, the Bureau of Reclamation (and a dozen other federal agencies) were busily conducting scores of expensive experiments *"to see if it worked."*

For bucking the government and trying to save Oklahoma farmers more than $250 million in drought losses, Krick was hauled before a Senate investigating committee.

Dr. Krick however, is lucky. He's making millions of dollars while proving that he was right. Others aren't that fortunate.

Because Immanuel Velikovsky (author of *Worlds in Collision* and several other volumes that presented evidence that the Earth experienced cosmic catastrophe only 3500 years ago) was right and orthodoxy dead wrong, the scientific Mafia conspired to break him. One of the great minds of modern times, Velikovsky was victimized by unfair censorship, public ridicule, and outright suppression of his first two books. Scientists ganged up to prevent further publication of the best-selling *Worlds in Collision* in 1950 by threatening to boycott Velikovsky's publisher (they were the writers of the majority of academic textbooks printed by Macmillan & Co.)

Unsatisfied at having "disgraced" him on the hallowed

grounds of academia, they sought to stop him from presenting his views directly to the American public. Under constant harrassment and ridicule, Velikovsky was forced to defend his revolutionary theory—that the world had undergone many global catastrophes in the historical past. The old scholar held his ground. Instead of accepting defeat, he carried on the fight in the most effective way—by publishing more books and presenting additional mountains of facts and evidence.

The hatred with which he is regarded is something of a record—even for long-lived grudge-holding. There's good reason for it, however. As the evidence from our space probes pours in, more and more young scientists are realizing that he was right all along. For this, the old-liners hate him all the more. Full acceptance of his theory would revolutionize every field of human knowledge and overthrow beliefs long accepted as axiomatic. It would also negate the erroneous conclusions of generations of scientists. And finally, it would revolutionize Man's fundamental concept of himself, his place in the Universe, and his fate.

Velikovsky *should have known* what it would cost him to advance such an overpoweringly unorthodox theory, and he probably did, but in the tradition of the true discoverer, he decided to follow the truth, regardless of where it led him. His correct predictions (blatant scientific "heresy" when first announced) are increasingly familiar to a new generation that has grown up with them. They are:

That the Sun itself is powerfully magnetically charged; that interplanetary space is permeated by the solar field; that "winds" of solar plasma exert a force; that Jupiter is a strong source of radio waves; that the Earth's magnetosphere extends to and beyond the Moon; that Venus is extremely hot, that it is rotating in retrograde motion—(the only planet in the solar system to do so); that the atmosphere of Venus consists of hydrocarbon gases, microbes, and possibly *insect life;* that Mars would be cratered and "more Moon-like than Earth-like"; and (of great importance to our future in space) *that Mars supports microorganisms of such virulence that they may be deadly to Man!*

The list of his accurate predictions is long and detailed. It almost seems as though Velikovsky was an eyewitness to the last destruction of all civilization on this planet. He correctly predicted that the Moon would be found to be "hot" inside, that hydrocarbons would be found on meteorites, that some of the world's great petroleum deposits are *not* millions of years old, but only a few *thousand,* that ash of extraterrestrial origin would be found on the floors of the oceans, that the Earth's axis has been displaced many times, that mastodons and mammoths roamed in great herds in Asia, Siberia, and America less than 3000 years ago, and that the classic peak of Meso-american civilization is a full thousand years older than the experts believed and taught.

The Russian-born, French-educated medical doctor studied biology, botany, and zoology at the University of Edinburgh; history, economics and law at Moscow's Free University; and later, psychology at the Brain Institute of Monokow in Vienna. For 15 years he practiced medicine and specialized in psychoanalysis in Jerusalem, Haifa, and Tel Aviv. Somehow, he also found time to launch a new scientific journal. His studies of "Freud's Heroes" (i.e., Akhenaten, Oedipus, and Moses) led him into the study of ancient cultures and a closer examination of events depicted in the scriptures, records, and sacred writings of all ancient people on Earth.

Everywhere he looked he found the same events reported on a global scale. Some universal catastrophe had befallen every civilization on the planet about 3500 years ago. Going further afield, he discovered even more concrete evidence supporting these reports in astronomy, geology, paleontology, physics, biology, botany, oceanography, and just about every discipline civilized man has developed.

For scientists to admit that much of the basis of modern science is a flimsy structure of unproven, often mistaken theories was entirely too much. "Velikovskyism" *had* to be stamped out!

In February 1974, the tall, 77-year-old heretic was invited to be the featured speaker at the annual meeting of the prestigious American Association for the Advancement of Science. This was only because of the clamor of a new, young generation of members. The battle-weary veteran strode to the speaker's podium and stood there; white-maned—as imposing as an Old Testament Patriarch—to receive a standing ovation from the younger, more conciliatory audience. But after 25 years of shabby treatment and personal abuse, the AAAS gesture was just a brief respite from the continuing storm of controversy, which has flared anew.

They're *still* at it; while the old man seems to be outliving his enemies, science has exacted its awful penalty. Ostracised like all other martyrs of sciencedom, Velikovsky *will* eventually be recognized—*posthumously*.

Some gratitude.

Nobody knows *how* many thousands of discoveries and inventions have been stifled, smothered and suppressed by Big Science. Even the most avid science booster has his doubts when confronted by the ugly but intolerable facts. This oppressive attitude has spread into our educational systems and the publication of textbooks. From their most susceptible days, schoolchildren are fed a constant diet of propaganda implying that the "Scientific Method" is as infallible as though it encompassed all *possible* ways of discovering truth. As a result, most of us grow up with a blind faith that science is some mysterious, almost magical system that always gets things done—even if we can't understand how.

The most successful scientists these days are executive types who are more familiar with stock market reports and corporate management systems than with the basic research or archeological field work. Only a small fraction of scientists are actually engaged in hard research. The rest, according to Dr. Norbert Weiner, the "father of cybernetics," are "scientific moppers-up after the true discoverers."

It may be that like human consciousness and evolution, the development of science is governed by higher laws.

Few people have a real understanding of what science is all about, and therein lies its chief weapon and our most dangerous delusion. The propaganda that it exists for your welfare and mine is pure fiction. Because of the amoral belief that science must compete for an ever-larger share of the military defense budget, there has been a growing wave of public disenchantment and outrage closely paralleling the growth of antiwar feeling.

"Mightier than the tread of marching armies is the power

of an idea whose time has come," wrote Victor Hugo. The phrase has a strange, absolute quality about it. Scientific discovery is *not* the sole province of an arrogant minority of self-appointed organizers and authoritarians. As soon as something as sensitive and personal as inspiration is organized, it is destroyed. The sooner they get the message, the better it will be for all of us.

There's no proof that God appointed the hierarchy of the Church to be His spokesmen. *Likewise, there are no exclusive spokesmen for Nature.*

Chapter Three

The Curse
of the Hope Diamond

Modern science refuses to credit Nature with any sense of direction or purpose—to say nothing of intelligence. Yet to reject the study of primary causes is to contradict the spirit of free scientific inquiry. According to Aristotle, "The wisdom for which all philosophers are in search is the knowledge of first principles and the causes of things."

Somewhere along the road to nineteenth and twentieth century materialism, science seems to have given up all hope of trying to comprehend primary cause; instead, it concentrates on secondary effects. Yet Nature seems to have deliberately created solid physical evidence indicating—if not the transcendent meaning of existence, then at least a path toward it.

There are forces and energies whose existence is still beyond our ability to detect or measure. Some of these radiations seem to be intimately connected with the Hope Diamond. If this most fabulous and beautiful of all gems actually does carry a "curse" (as legend and record indicate), what possible "Mechanism" could there be for it? How would such a thing work? Are we even *capable* of understanding it? The diamond exists; its history is real, not a series of "coincidences."

Like gravity and telepathy, the deeper meaning of electricity and magnetism, which affect every living thing, remain almost total mysteries to modern science. But we're now on the brink of new ways of sensing and measuring forces that were undreamed of just a few short years ago. Minerologists have discovered that the Hope Diamond does indeed transmit subtle emanations. Some of these seem to lie *beyond* the detectable electromagnetic spectrum because, like telepathy and gravity, they act at a distance and penetrate all obstacles, *including a Faraday cage,* which screens all E+M radiation.

Here is the factual and scientific story of the known history of the world's most fabulous diamond:

At 11 o'clock on the morning of November 18, 1958, James G. Todd, a smartly uniformed postman, delivered a small brown package to the Smithsonian Institution in Washington, D.C. It contained the most fabulous and best known gem on Earth, and was insured for a million dollars. Harry Winston, one of America's famous jewelers, had just presented the Hope Diamond to the government of the United States.

Some observers don't think he did us any favor. "There's a long and bloody history behind the Hope Diamond," observed Dr. George Switzer, curator of mineral sciences at the Smithsonian, "but we're hoping the curse has now ended."

Not everyone thinks so, including columnist Art Buchwald, who wrote (with tongue in cheek, no doubt), "The Hope Diamond has brought nothing but grief to anyone who ever owned it. Whoever accepted it on behalf of the United States did this country a great disservice."

Jeweler Harry Winston, however, seems to have nothing but scorn for the stone's legendary curse. "I wanted to start a jewel room in Washington," he said when asked why he donated the treasure piece to the United States. "Other nations have them and, after all, the Hope is the best known and most beautiful diamond on Earth. It's like a lovely day in June ... so soft, so blue—it isn't cold, you know. It lives. It talks to you. It sings."

Be that as it may, the song it sang to postman James Todd, who delivered the stone to the Smithsonian, was a tragic dirge. Not long after he turned the diamond over to Dr. Switzer's office, he was struck by a series of calamities. It all began when his home in Seat Pleasant, Maryland, was gutted by fire, and his favorite dog strangled to death on her leash. Next, Todd was thrown from his car and suffered a serious head injury. Shortly afterward, his leg was crushed by a truck, and finally his wife, the mother of his four children, died of a heart attack—*all within two short weeks of delivery of the Hope Diamond!*

Whether it was "curse" or coincidence, the fact remains that the Hope Diamond is the most *scientifically* unique object in the annals of minerology. Since it was installed in a display case under the protection of armed guards and electronic surveillance, millions of visitors have come to gaze and marvel at Uncle Sam's exotic bauble. One look will convince the hardest skeptic that Winston was right: this blue-violet stone is unparalled for its sheer purity and beauty.

A few years ago when the Smithsonian loaned the gem to the De Beers Consolidated Mines in Johannesburg, South Africa, for a series of scientific tests, they discovered that it is *the only known blue diamond* that glows like a red-hot coal when exposed to ultraviolet light. "No such phenomenon has ever been recorded before for blue diamonds," said Dr. Switzer. "All other diamonds of this type give off a pale blue color when bombarded with untraviolet."

Several curious gem sleuths are still searching for a couple of smaller pieces believed to have been chipped off the original, larger version of the 44½-carat Hope. The "French Blue," as it was then known, weighed 67½ carats. The pieces *should* be recognizable, the experts reason, by their red glow when exposed to ultraviolet light.

Most large, expensive gems come ready equipped with stories that range from the bizarre to the incredible. The history of the Hope Diamond, however, is one of the most convoluted blends of fact and legend on record. Ever since it emerged from the relative obscurity of Burma by way of India three centuries ago it has been associated with what must be a world's record for death and disaster. According to legend, the Brahmin priest who helped to pluck the stone from the golden forehead of the idol Rama Sita was tortured to death for his part in the theft.

Possibly because of today's increased interest in almost anything occult, the fact that the Hope Diamond glows red and conducts enormous amounts of electricity (far more than any other stone of its kind), has given additional credence to its legendary "curse."

The list of death, disaster, and ruin associated with the Hope Diamond—without embellishment, and whether or not you subscribe to its "curse"—is truly impressive:

A Folies Bergère star who wore it was murdered by her lover. A Greek broker who bought it drove off a cliff and was crushed in his car with his wife and children. Several governments which owned it eventually fell upon troubled times, faced collapse and even ruin.

Long before it ever became the Hope Diamond extraordinary atrocities were committed to acquire the gem. In its original form the Blue Diamond weighed 112½ carats (before cutting and polishing). Afterward, its weight was reduced by 45 carats to 67½ carats. Even then it was still a lovely deep blue color, the rarest, most exquisite and flawless stone of its kind in the world. One minerologist suggested that a scientific case might be made for the theory that the Hope Diamond's red glow may—in some as-yet-mysterious way—be connected to its evil history.

It has certainly inspired intense greed. Men have dug holes in their own bodies to hide it. Legend has it that the Blue was once found in the stomach of a buried human corpse. (A messenger had attempted to steal it while delivering it, but was intercepted by still other thieves who brutally murdered him and then used his body as a hiding place.)

Gruesome as they are, such tales are fairly typical folklore for many of the world's famous gems. Whatever may be said of the Blue's history from the time it was stolen from Rama Sita, the authentic account (which began with a strange keeper of royal gems) is spellbinding. An infamous French jewel expert named Jean Baptiste Tavernier, who was the guardian of the king's treasures, engineered the theft of the stone from Rama Sita, the statue of which stood in the most holy temple in the ancient city of Pagan in Burma.

Hero or villain, Tavernier was a most remarkable man. While most of his contemporaries were either in their dotage or their graves, the octogenarian was plotting to steal the Blue Diamond by patiently following an intricate plan. He gained the confidence of the last of the great Indian Moguls, Emperor Aurangzeb, and through him the priests of the temple of Rama Sita.

Surrounding himself with ostentatious luxury, Tavernier made a point of visiting the Pagan temple with his retinue of servants each day. And each day he placed a precious gem—*of moderate value*—at the stone feet of Rama Sita while pretending to worship the idol. At last, when the priests' confidence in him was established and unquestioned, Tavernier and his hired thugs surprised the last remaining guard on duty, and bound and gagged him. They then pried the matchless Blue Diamond from the idol's head and—according to involved preplanning—fled the country.

When the theft was discovered and the insiders who had helped Tavernier were caught and punished, the Great Mogul and his priests are reported to have held a ceremonial meeting. According to legend, they prayed that the "outraged" Rama Sita would follow anyone who should ever possess the Blue Diamond and wreak his terrible vengeance upon him. In the minds of millions of people, the diamond's long and bloody history is proof enough that the stone does carry an awesome curse.

There are gaps and inconsistencies in the story thus far, but when he returned from his sixth voyage to India in 1668, the aged but still conniving Frenchman brought the 112½-carat Blue Diamond to France, where, with great ingenuity, he presented it to Louis XIV. The king rewarded him with a lavish fortune and a much-coveted title of nobility.

Next, Tavernier sold the great half-egg Mogul Diamond to Catherine the Great and was once more returning to France (this time by way of the steppes of Russia) when a pack of ravenous wolves attacked his party. As the sole survivor of the ill-fated expedition told it, the voracious animals devoured Tavernier and his companions. Subsequent history throws a different light on the tragedy; it is now considered extremely doubtful that wolves attack and eat people. Tavernier was probably murdered for whatever treasure he may have had at the time.

This is where the most reliable history of the rarest stone actually begins. The Blue was subsequently cut down to a 67½-carat pear-shaped pendant which was frequently seen gracing the ample bosom of Madame de Montespan. But when Louis XIV's love for his mistress turned to jealousy and finally bitter hatred, he callously rejected her. Not long afterward, he contracted smallpox. Then, bit by bit, his once gloriously successful reign ended in a humiliating series of political, military, and personal defeats.

From time to time the lovely Princess de Lamballe wore the diamond, which was now called the "French Blue." During the French Revolution she was beaten to death by an uncontrollable mob. The maddened horde of screaming revolutionaries hacked off her head, mounted it on a pointed pole and paraded it in full view of her closest friend, Marie Antoinette. Marie (who had also worn the Blue) and Louis XVI met their end at the hands of the republican rabble; both lost their heads.

The crown jewels of France, including the Blue, were quickly confiscated by the new regime of the people. Their leaders generously placed the gems on display for the edification of the populace every Monday in a large hall at the Garde-Meubles. Today it is an ordinary hotel in the Place de la Concorde.

On the moonloss night of September 16, 1792, a gangster named Miette and his gang of 22 pulled the biggest coup of their lives by stealing all the crown jewels, including the famed Regent and the Blue Diamond. The combination of the rich booty and the fantastic success of the robbery had a strange effect on the gang leader. Almost overnight he became arrogant and cocky about his great accomplishment. He began telling secrets and making enemies. He also made the tactical error of dumping his old flame, a willful, passionate brunette named Citoyenne Corbin, for another woman. Jealous and angry, Citoyenne betrayed her former lover and his entire gang to the police, thus avenging herself and acquiring a sizable reward for her trouble.

Twenty of Miette's gang were arrested; 15 were given life sentences—to be served in dungeons. The other five were sent to the guillotine and beheaded. On the information provided by Citoyenne all the jewels (with the single exception of the French Blue) were recovered from a filthy alley ditch along the Champs-Élysées.

According to a 1791 inventory of the French crown jewels, the Blue Diamond ranked second only to the Regent in value. The latter, which was found hidden in an attic beam of an old home, was worth 480,000 pounds; the Blue, 120,000.

When the French Republic found itself in desperate need of money it transferred the Regent Diamond to Switzerland as security for a large loan. Napoleon eventually redeemed it and had it set in his sword of state. Until that moment, fortune had generally sided with Bonaparte, who soon suffered his famous defeat at Waterloo.

The Blue Diamond mysteriously disappeared for several years, but rumors and speculation about obscure crimes, including murder, surround the stone. It finally turned up in the possession of a Dutch diamond cutter named Wilhelm Fals, who died of sheer grief when his own son, Hendrick, stole it from him.

Hendrick later committed suicide.

History records the next possessor of the Blue as Francois Beaulieu, a cowardly man who knew about the terrible curse and died a thousand deaths in fear of what might happen to him. In order to change what he felt was a dire fate, he had a fairly large chip cut off the stone. *(To this day, no one seems to know what became of that chip.)* The French Blue was now slightly oblong, but was still too well known to be sold either in Paris or Amsterdam. Beaulieu skulked the streets of London in perpetual hunger, rage, fear, and sleeplessness—with a king's ransom sewn into his filthy rags.

In order to survive he took a menial job and probably became the richest street sweeper in history. Living in near despair, Beaulieu finally screwed up enough courage to try selling the accursed stone. He finally accepted a piddling 5,000 pounds from a shifty English jewel dealer named Danile Eliason. But when thieves stole all his money, Beaulieu simply disappeared.

When the French Blue reappeared in Eliason's possession, still another piece had been chipped from it; its corners were rounded and it was reduced by 23 carats to its present 44½ carats—*a tremendous loss of weight*. At best, the legitimate diamond dealers of the day were extremely suspicious of the Blue Diamond's apparent lack of pedigree. Moreover, they considered Eliason a shady character who couldn't provide a plausible history for the fabulous stone. But they were soon convinced that this was indeed all that remained of the French Blue.

In 1830 Eliason—his reputation almost ruined, his health impaired, and most of his money gone—managed to sell the gem to the English banker Henry Thomas Hope for a reputed 90,000 pounds. (Some experts dispute this and claim that the price was only 18,000 pounds, which—except for the stone's terrible legacy—would normally have been considered a terrific bargain.) Running true to its historical form, the Blue Diamond was so devastatingly effective in the dissipation of the Hope family's fortune that gem watchers and believers in the curse renamed it in honor of three generations of Hopes. It passed through the hands of a son, a nephew, and a grandson, ruining them one by one.

Henry T. Hope's son actually changed his name in a desperate attempt to sidestep further disaster. In spite of this tacit superstition he lost everything he had—including the diamond. As soon as he was bereft his wife left him and ran off with another man. The Hope Diamond was then passed on to another relative, and he too was wiped out financially.

Some gem experts are convinced that two smaller blue diamonds were part of the larger French Blue before it was cut up. One of these stones, exactly the same color as the Hope Diamond (a pear-shaped gem weighing 13¾ carats), was acquired by the Duke of Brunswick. He also experienced a series of misfortunes which were reminiscent of those that befell owners of the Hope Diamond and he was forced to sell everything he owned at an auction in Geneva in April 1874.

In hot pursuit of this clue, gem expert Edwin W. Streeter made a truly remarkable discovery: still *another* exact duplicate of the French Blue's unique color which he found in the newly acquired stock of a dealer. It was considerably smaller, but it also had a sporadic history of misery and misfortune. Streeter thoroughly checked the Brunswick diamond against the smaller stone and concluded that the mystery of the French Blue's pieces was finally solved.*

The next member of the Hope family to inherit the Blue Diamond happened to be a member of Parliament. So convinced (and terrified) was he of the stone's evil properties that he made a fast transaction and sold it to the Duchess of

*Edwin W. Streeter, *Great Diamonds of the World.*

45

Newcastle for 25,000 pounds. The Duchess however, had a bright idea or two of her own about the diamond; she managed to unload it in one of the speediest deals on record—to an unsuspecting (or disbelieving) New York jeweler named Joseph Frankel.

The ink had barely had time to dry on the transaction papers when Frankel began to experience the worst possible financial troubles. In a few months he managed to lose all the wealth he had spent his entire life accumulating. He finally put the Hope Diamond on a Paris auction block where a French jeweler named Jacques Calot bought it.

Calot went insane and committed suicide.

The next owner was a Russian prince named Ivan Kanitovski. He was stabbed to death. Rumor has it that Catherine the Great also wore it before she died of "apoplexy."

The gem's awful history continued unabated. One of its owners was reported to be a German lady who lived in royal style for a short time, then was reduced to working as a scrubwoman in a shipyard for $2 a day. Next, a Spaniard who owned the Hope Diamond was shipwrecked and drowned. A Greek broker who sold it to a Turkish sultan was killed along with his family when his car crashed through a fence and plummeted in flames down a mountain ravine. The sultan, Abdul Hamid, paid $400,000 for the jewel, which he then presented to his favorite wife. She must have been nursing an old grudge because she stabbed him. Not enough to kill him; but then his government began to disintegrate under the onslaught of The Young Turks Revolt. Realizing now that the end of his reign and everything he was familiar with was near, the sultan dispatched his agents to Paris in order to sell his collection of gems—which included the Hope Diamond—for as much as they could raise.

Long before the sultan's troubles began, a Washington, D.C. socialite, who was one of the few women from the Western world who had ever visited the inner sanctum of the Turkish court, saw the great gem gleaming from the Sultan's lavish turban, and dreamed of one day possessing it. In Janaury 1911, Evelyn Walsh McLean formally acquired the gem for $112,000 in Washington, D.C.

The gem was still new to the McLeans when their son was

killed in a strange automobile accident that was never fully explained. Next, their daughter became exceedingly morose and committed suicide with an overdose of sleeping pills. The loss of his children capped a series of personal setbacks for Edward McLean, who couldn't bear up to the double tragedy. He suffered a nervous breakdown and, hopelessly insane, died in a mental institution.

Despite the fears of her friends and relatives, Mrs. McLean obstinately refused to part with her diamond. She seemed to be immune to its terrible influence, which prompted the belief that the Blue (like the Koh-i-noor, the Regent, and several other famous diamonds) worked its worst evil almost entirely on men. Mrs. McLean also happened to use the gem unselfishly. In the early 1930s she pawned it for enough money to ransom the kidnapped Lindbergh baby and often displayed it to wounded veterans at the Walter Reed Hospital.

Evelyn McLean died in 1947, a legend in her own time. When the family estate was put up for sale, millionaire Harry Winston bought everything—including the Hope Diamond— for a million dollars. For awhile, Winston followed the example of Mrs. McLean and carefully displayed the fabulous gem at bazaars and charity shows. No one knows why the shrewd businessman encountered such a series of financial reversals during the next decade or whether he actually gave any currency to the diamond's strange history.

Whichever it was, he invested $143 for insurance totaling $1 million, plus $2 for postage, and had the diamond delivered to the Smithsonian in 1958.

Except for rare excursions such as the trip made for scientific tests by the De Beers people in South Africa, the Hope Diamond, now a national American treasure, remains on constant display in a heavily guarded glass case in the nation's capital.

Is the Hope Diamond radiating some strange, undiscovered kind of energy—something apart from the electromagnetic spectrum as we know it? This is the interesting question raised by atomic scientists who can now bombard clear white diamonds with subatomic particles in a cyclotron. These bombardments *permanently* change the color of white diamonds to pink, green, and blue tints. *Why* does the Hope Diamond glow red when exposed to ultraviolet light? It is possible for an inanimate object that conducts electricity to have some kind of effect on a living creature—a human being?

"Almost anything is *conceivable*," said Dr. George Switzer, the Smithsonian's chief minerologist. "Look, all life is carbon-based, and diamonds are the hardest, purest, most densely compacted form of carbon; they also conduct electricity, so there might be some kind of energy exchange between a human being and a diamond. I don't say there *is*, but we're just beginning to learn new things about radiation and magnetism that we never knew before. Who can predict how far this knowledge will take us?"

It seems unlikely that scientists would investigate anything as bizarre as an "accursed" gem, no matter how weighty the evidence or how tantalizing the implications may be. The evidence *and* its implications are, to them, "irrational." Parapsychologists are having a difficult enough time trying to learn how sensitives such as Peter Hurkos can get "psychic readings" or impressions from inanimate objects. "If a piece of gold, a watch or a jewel has some mysterious way of 'charging' itself with a kind of energy (analogous to the way a steel bar is magnetized, perhaps) and then 'playing it back' or *releasing it on demand*," says G. Henry Stein, a research scientist for Flow Technology, Inc., "today's Scientific Method would never uncover it."

Stein, a friendly, intensely-true-to-the-*real*-scientific-method scientist, rubbed his jet-black crew cut and grimaced. "Damn! I *know* there are other kinds of energy. I've *seen* it work. We haven't even become aware of the forces that influence us yet. I think it may be possible for a diamond (or anything else for that matter) to retain and later release various kinds of energy fields. Maybe it soaks up human hatred and fear and then releases it under the right circumstances," he said.

Whatever the explanation for the incredible series of coincidences—whether it's strictly scientific or the mythical vengeance of Rama Sita and his priests—the Hope Diamond remains one of history's greatest mysteries. "So far," said the Smithsonian's Dr. George Switzer, "no one has studied it under an electron scanning microscope. There may be further surprises in store."

Another gem expert suggested that "Kirlian photographs might reveal the extent of whatever the stone is emanating—or generating." If this theory has any basis, it would seem to suggest that the Hope Diamond has a kind of "life"—not as we know it, perhaps, but as a subminiature kind of planet such as Jupiter (which radiates radio waves and a powerful electromagnetic field), Earth, or Mars, which also influence life forms.

When the science of psionics has finally been recognized as a valid field for orthodox researchers, it might be interesting to see whether a psionic device such as the Hieronymus Machine can detect the Hope Diamond's alleged evil influence.

Chapter Four

The Incredible Hieronymus Machine

Flying high over the peaceful, rolling hills and lush farm-land of the Cumberland Valley near the Pennsylvania Dutch Country, the converted military reconnaissance aircraft's wing-mounted cameras faithfully recorded thousands of acres below where the precious crops were being attacked by countless hordes of hungry insects.

The men who'd chartered the plane developed the film and showed it to one of the local farmers. He outlined the blighted areas of his farm in ink, spreading patches of brown-ish-gray. A young technician from the Homeotronic Research Foundation in Newport, Pa. scissored out the sections the farmer had indicated, and kept the negatives. Then he placed the selected cuts in the small well of a strange-looking black box with dials on the outside and some kind of electronic-looking circuitry inside. An electric cord on the box was plugged into an outdoor socket.

"Turn this large dial on the top all the way to the right," the technician instructed the farmer, "every morning from 8:30 to 11 for a week."

Several days passed before the farmer and the owners of the black box device inspected the "treated" areas. They found that virtually every corn borer, Japanese beetle, and even the nematodes in the soil of the outlined areas were completely dead—exterminated in some strange manner by "something"—a nonelectronic power or force from the box.

In central Florida a few months later, Dr. William J. Hale, then chief of Dow Chemical Company research, photo-graphed a blighted citrus orchard. He painted the *pictures* of several rows of infected trees with a chemical that was deadly to the insects, in this case, the slender, threadlike nematodes, which in a warm climate are among the world's most destructive and ineradicable parasites. They bore into the soil to depths of 10 to 14 feet and are perfectly immune to the most deadly pesticides.

Dow's chief chemist placed the photograph into a device that looked almost identical to that used in Pennsylvania and instructed the citrus grower as follows: "Turn this big dial all the way to the right for two hours every morning." This particular machine *seemed* to be electronically powered, but there was no visible power source.

One week later, every *second* row—the areas Dr. Hale had painted with the chemical reagent *in the photograph*—was free of the parasitic infestation. Uncountable numbers of dead nematodes deep in the soil, unreachable by ordinary means, had been killed by some invisible force from the "machine" in the soil that had been their haven and breeding ground.

The extermination of insects—*at a distance and without pesticides*—at the Municipal Works in Rosenheim, West Germany, was also reported in detail in the November 3, 1969, issue of the *Journal of Paraphysics*. Similar experiments in California and Arizona were conducted by members of the Homeotronic Research Foundation. Fifty thousand acres of diseased and insect infested trees were treated successfully.

In this "biotonic" treatment, the "resonant point of contact" was a leaf or some sap from a plant or tree. In the same way, people have been treated with these psionics machines; among humans, a sample of blood, a lock of hair, or a skin scraping have been used to establish the "link" to the patient. Even a photograph can be used effectively—*as long as the negative isn't destroyed!*

Impossible? Of course it is—according to the "known and accepted laws of science." But science couldn't possibly know all the laws that exist in the Universe. In fact, by the discovery of a completely new and different kind of energy or force, researchers learned that the scientific method doesn't always work!

In 1950 a man named J. P. Boyce of Victorville, California, was invited to visit the helpless owners of a huge expanse of cotton in Arizona near Tucson called the Cortaro

Farms. Despite heavy crop dusting on a wholesale basis, the cotton growers were being eaten out of several million dollars by boll weevils. They were desperate, so when they heard the fantastic stories about Boyce's "magic box" they decided to try it.

Here's part of a feature story written by Norman Harrington for the Tucson *Daily Citizen* about what happened:*

"The management of the Cortaro farms gave Boyce an 80-acre plot of cotton to work on and sat back to watch the results.

"Here's where the story becomes more fantastic!

"First, this man took an aerial photo of the 80-acre field. He then determined what insects were likely to strike the cotton field and selected a natural repellent. Science says that every known insect has a 'natural' repellent, so this is fairly easy to determine.

"Then the man brought out a small piece of radio-like equipment built in a piece of aluminum luggage. He grounded the gadget and extended a whip-antenna some eight to ten feet in the air. He turned the thing on for a few minutes and then packed it up and left.

"He returned twice a week during the bug season and performed the same operation. He talked several other cotton growers in the area into allowing him to treat their fields of growing cotton and each job was handled in a similar fashion.

"In nearby fields the crop dusting planes were at work day after day dropping their clouds of death-dealing fog on the pesky insects, but in the treated fields all was quiet and peaceful with the bees humming happily and the butterflies flitting from one blossom to another.

"And, to the surprise of everyone—except the man with the gadget—there were no plant-destroying or boll-destroying insects in the treated fields.

"The cotton in these fields seemed to be stronger and the bolls seemed to have more seed. The crop from the treated acres looks like a bumper harvest. More cotton for less money.

*Tucson *Daily Citizen*, October 3, 1950.

"Truly—a push-button war on bugs.

"At this point," Harrington conceded, "you have a right to ask—'How does it work?' My only answer is to attempt to explain the process as it was told to me in an hour and a half by J. P. Boyce of Victorville, Calif.—the man with the 'thing.'

"The photo negative of the field being treated was inserted in the machine to determine the basic carrier wave released by the machine. That localizes the treatment to one plot of land. Then the natural repellent is inserted into another part of the machine so that its wave length is transmitted out on the basic carrier wave of the field. The process is much the same as that employed in modern radio broadcasting where speech or music is transmitted on a certain wavelength that can be picked up by a receiving set.

"Here's where the machine goes to work: the insect has picked its lunch by reacting to the plant wave-length that attracts its appetite. In the area of the plot of ground covered by the negative the machine releases a signal which strikes an *unresponsive* chord in the bug and he sails right on by seeking food elsewhere . . ."

We-e-e-e-l-l-l, Harrington had only an hour and a half with this man, so his description lacks a few fine details—such as the fact that the machine can *kill*.

But it's an ill wind that doesn't have some cooling influence. Psionic machines can also heal and cure, often by thoroughly mystifying means. It's easier to grasp an idea like this when it's first applied to lower animals or—in this case—plants. A group of the psionic researchers in Pennsylvania demonstrated—in a most unusual experiment—that the *future* condition of an organism can be detected electronically *and photographically!* (In the next chapter on electrodynamic fields, you'll see scientific evidence amounting to virtual proof of the existence of the human "aura" or L-field.)

These experimenters placed a lily seed in the well of one of their psionic devices—this one patterned after the Delawarr camera in England. After the plate was developed, the experimenters were exuberant; the *bulb* cycle of the life potential in the lily seed was revealed as an extraordinarily clear X-ray picture! Using the same seed, the man operating the camera *concentrated* on a still later period in the lily's life cycle and, while "tuning" to the correct vibrational rate, developed another photograph (totally *different* from Kirlian photography) in which the fully developed lily was flowering!

At the laboratories of George de la Warr in Oxford, England, a white-coated lab technician placed a few drops of a woman's *blood* into the receptacle of an odd-looking device full of interior lenses, coils, and prisms—in effect, an inside-out camera. While concentrating intently, he turned a series of dials and stroked a flat plate. An assistant loaded a photographic plate into a side slot. Silently, they timed the exposure. The developed picture was *a profile view of a woman's lower vetebrae and pelvic region.* A semitransparent human fetus was clearly visible.

"She's about 10 to 12 weeks along, I'd say," one lab tech guessed.

"That's about right. Let's see if it progresses normally; do you suppose we could see it at five or six months . . .?"

They could, and did. All over the world there's a new kind of excitement, a spirit of adventure beyond the wildest dreams of Arabian Nights fanciers. It's expanding and accelerating with enormous speed and enthusiasm. Both at the government and academic levels hardly a month goes by without three or four announcements of important national and international forums discussing previously unheard-of theories.

New York University, for example, held a conference in May, 1974, titled, "Focusing New Energies." Some of the topics: "Bioenergetics: In Search of our Living Force"; "The Energy Field (Aura) In Man and Nature"; "Psychic Aspects of Healing"; "The New Way of Seeking and Knowing", and dozens of similar topics. The experts ranged from Al Huang to John Pierrakos to Andrija Puharich, all renowned names in parapsychology.

"There's a new force, an energy connected with people," wrote Lynn Schroeder and Shelia Ostrander in *Psychic Discoveries Behind the Iron Curtain,* "an energy known or unknown that can be directed by mind. That's why interest is running high . . . why even the Soviets are trying to find the general laws behind spectacular feats (*such as bending met-*

al with mind power, making objects sail through the air, killing live organisms at long range, tracing and locating foreign agents in distant cities from their photographs alone), just as flying a kite to catch a spark of lightning is important only because it led to the discovery of the ... laws of electricity."

All available evidence indicates that the human race may be teetering on the brink of a series of discoveries that dwarf the combined invention of the wheel or the discovery of fire, electricity—*and* atomic energy!

"My personal hunch," said John W. Campbell, Jr., in one of his *Astounding Science Fact-Fiction* editorials in 1956, "is that these individuals and groups are prodding at the edges of a new field that will open a totally new concept of the Universe. And that, within the next 20 years, the barrier will be cracked: a reproducible machine will be achieved when a valid theory of operation is achieved—and not before. But I believe that that can be, and *will* be done before 1976."

One of the men he considered most likely to make the breakthrough in psionics *is* T. Galen Hieronymus, a remarkable inventor whose creative life extends over six decades. Hieronymus started developing new methods of broadcast techniques during 1919–20 when he was in the Army Signal Corps as a radio operator and electrical engineer with the Rainbow Division in France. The young Hieronymus had his own ham radio license and was with station KDKA in Pittsburgh, Pennsylvania, in 1913 where he took part in the first radio broadcast.

While trying to develop a wireless telephone during the early days of World War I, he discovered some peculiar properties of certain metals and minerals. This led him to experiment with psionics, which was then called *radionics* or *radiesthesia*, a kind of higher-echelon "dowsing" with different instruments to detect abnormal changes in the human body. The most valuable pioneering work and discovery in psionics was done by a well-to-do and brilliant San Francisco physician, Dr. Albert Abrams, between 1886 and 1924. Hieronymus doesn't say how much he was influenced by Abrams' work, but he was inspired by early psionics pioneers.

In 1956 Hieronymus presented John Campbell with a copy

of his patent; it was precisely the sort of device the editor of *Astounding* had written about. The inventor had applied for it in 1946, and after considerable debate, received his patent number in 1948.

But Hieronymus was very careful to introduce his device simply as an instrument for detecting "emanations from inert matter," mainly minerals. For reasons best known to himself, Hieronymus deliberately kept the life-affecting capacities of his device a well-kept secret.

At about the same time in Oxford, England, another psionics researcher, George De la Warr, made the startling discovery that the emulsion on a photographic plate was somehow linked to the person whose photograph was taken—or to anything or anyone else in the photograph.

If this had been the *only* discovery of its kind, the total skepticism of orthodox medical experts would be understandable, but it wasn't. Dozens (perhaps scores) of others were performing identical experiments in America, England, France, Germany, and Australia. (Hardly anyone knew it then, but their Soviet counterparts were already engaged in *official* psionics research programs.)

But most Western scientists shrugged off the reports as though they were the brainchildren of crackpot inventors, "magic," ritualistic superstition masquerading as science and camouflaged with nonfunctional electronic "props." The American Medical Association called it "voodoo" and classified it with the use of *placebos*—the medical practice of dispensing harmless pills composed of sugar or some "inert" substance when a doctor believes the patient's illness is imaginary. In most cases, it works, and the symptoms disappear—IF the patient's illness is "all in his mind."

In a way, it involves or invokes the Laws of Sympathetic Magic wherein "the Symbol *is* the Object (both in its present actuality and its future potentiality). *Therefore,* whatever is done to the Symbol also happens to the Object."

It's perfectly understandable, of course, that an impressionable patient who is confronted with a brisk, highly professional expert who subjects him to probes and treatments with a lot of incomprehensible (to him) electronic machinery would be susceptible enough to trigger equally incomprehensible inner abilities to fight off his illness or disease—even cancer. Hypnotists have known of thousands of such cases. There's now growing evidence among orthodox medical men who are engaged in psychosomatic studies that even terminally ill cancer patients can be taught to cure themselves through meditation.

The "charlatans" and "quacks" supposedly practicing voodoo on the desperate and gullible would have to include parapsychologists of the Soviet Academy of Sciences. Unlike the vast majority of their Western colleagues, Russian scientists simply assume the reality of apparent supranormal phenomena such as telepathy, clairvoyance, psychokinesis (the ability to move physical objects with the power of mind alone), and even interplanetary telepathy—and are trying to learn everything they can about it.

British and American scientific institutions, by and large, insist that an "acceptable" theory must precede any experimentation. It's Catch 22: even though you can demonstrate the existence of a new kind of force, power or energy, they won't look unless you have a perfectly logical and therefore (scientifically) "acceptable" explanation of how it works.

At the moment, *nobody* knows *how* it works—that it works is eminently evidential. Psionics researchers who are 1) patriotic, and 2) highly security conscious, fear that the stakes are simply too high to deal with in the manner of "business as usual." High-risk national security matters, or *ESP*ionage, as it's often called, would profit immensely through the perfection of a constantly reliable electronic device that would amplify and control the mind's powers—especially of psychokinesis.*

When you come right down to it, it makes relatively little difference whether you establish a link between a man and his photograph or use the photo of, for example, an intelligence agent to pinpoint his location (or cause his death) anywhere on the planet. This isn't just a fanciful notion; it's been done openly, not only on Earth, but with men in space as well. With this device, T. Galen Hieronymus "eavesdropped"

---

*I have it from several reliable sources that an incredibly sophisticated form of "Psionic Warfare" is now being conducted by *at least* four major world powers—J.F.G. 3–4–75.

on the space flight of Apollo 8 and was so successful with the "photographic-tuning" ability of his machine that he and his wife, Louise, published a series of his own medical reports on the Mitogenic Radiations (also called Helioda Waves, Eloptic Emanations, or Odic Force) of all the Apollo astronauts from then on. He closely monitored their physiological conditions and changes throughout the lunar voyage and return—even after splash down and during the ensuing quarantine periods.

What was most important and significant of all, the test data from Hieronymus' device completely agreed with NASA's own medical telemetry systems. Hieronymus got a leg up on the space medics, however, when he detected the presence of a mysterious belt of radiation surrounding the Moon.

"This radiation," claims the inventor, "is harmful—*possibly deadly*—to human beings."

To date, no one has stayed on the Moon long enough to find out just how deadly this force may be, but there could be obstacles to future science colonies to overcome among the lunar maria ("seas"). "We're beginning to find hidden barriers and limitations in unexpected places," he insists, "humans are rather adaptable creatures . . . *on Earth*. But what kind of forces will we find in other planetary environments?"

Aside from the noxious Venusian carbon dioxide or Jupiter's deadly methane and ammonia atmospheres, little or no consideration has been given to the possibility of invisible but lethal fields surrounding other worlds. Of course, Hieronymus, de la Warr, Ruth Drown, and others know how people respond to the *Earth's* magnetic field, to the steady, gentle pull of gravity and even higher octaves of more refined energies.

"Every living thing radiates this Odic Force," said Baron von Reichenbach (the famous chemist who invented creosote and scores of related chemicals). He was so impressed by the pioneering work of Dr. Albert Abrams* and Dr. Franz A. Mesmer of "animal magnetism" fame that he devoted his life to the study and practice of radionics.

*Albert Abrams, M.D., *New Concepts in Diagnosis and Treatment.* The Philopolis Press, San Francisco, 1916.

"The energy pattern from a patient's blood specimen," said Dr. Albert Abrams, "is in permanent resonance with the body it came from."

How? Through what medium?

"All things in the Universe are interdependent, and in radionics all things are related—not in a physical sense, but through another dimension which we are not yet able to describe," he said. "Materialism confines us to three dimensions. All forms of matter possess a quality hitherto unsuspected that puts them in touch with each other's signals."

Dr. Abrams was born in San Francisco in 1865 and graduated with honors from the University of Heidelberg. He later became professor of pathology at Stanford University where he continued to build and test magnetic and electrical devices to detect disease in living tissue. Though his work was not well received, he managed to invent a variety of radionic instruments that were far ahead of their time—so much so, that it took the discovery of the Fields of Life to help put psionics in its proper perspective.

"No matter how small or diluted it may be, there's a resonance between the whole human body and each of its parts," said Ruth Drown, inventor of a radionics receiver-transmitter device, prior to her death after a brief stint in a West Coast Prison for "fraud." The hostile American Medical Association protested about her methods and devices, and she was charged and convicted for fraud and medical quackery. Her device, of course, was declared a hoax by the American Medical Association's legal experts. The AMA had merely heard *about* reports from cured patients, but did not conduct tests of its own.

Oddly enough, even the blood of identical twins is different enough to emit a dissimilar "resonance." The body as a whole emanates a characteristic sonorousness. In his book *New Worlds Beyond the Atom,** Langston Day said: "After discovering that the emulsion of an ordinary photographic plate is somehow linked to the person in the photograph, we found that the same rule applied to plants. Later we discovered that plant growth could be stimulated by color irradia-

---

*Langston Day with George de la Warr, *New Worlds Beyond the Atom.* Vincent Stuart, Ltd., London, 1956.

tion from a distance—*indirectly,* that is, by bathing the *photograph* of the plant with light . . .

"How can there be a link between a plant and its photograph?" he wondered. "The image on the plate is formed by the multiplicity of reflected light rays coming from the cabbage," De la Warr explained. "But in addition to light, other kinds of vital radiations are also emanating from the cabbage; these are received by the emulsion.

". . . Each molecule of matter carries an electric charge which is specific for that particular molecule; this charge acts as an inconceivably tiny radio station which both transmits and receives its own particular signals. When these countless myriads of charged molecules are broadcasting, they build a Generic Pattern which is the means whereby form or shape appears in the material world.

"The *combined* signal from a plant or a human being, a signal composed of the separate broadcasts of the billions of charged molecules which compose it, is unique. The cabbage in your larder is not quite the same as any other cabbage, and 'Mr. Brown,' for example, is a little different in his physical makeup from any other man in the world. In the same way, the signals broadcast from this cabbage, or from 'Mr. Brown,' are different from any other broadcast signals.

"Furthermore, since each tiny molecular change is also a *receiving station,* the Generic Pattern of a plant or a human being governs the pattern of signals received from outside. This is where a photograph plays its part. The emulsion retains the Generic Pattern of the thing which is photographed, and therefore it acts as a tuned transmitter. If a radionic broadcast is projected through it, this Generic Pattern will transmit exactly the pattern of radiations suitable for affecting the plant (or human being) at a distance."

When Ed Hermann, an engineer at McGraw-Hill, the New York-based publishing company, requested that Hieronymus treat a caterpillar-infested tree on his lawn, he never expected anything as far-out as "long-distance extermination." Everything else he'd tried had failed however. For several years, and in spite of all the pesticides he and his neighbors used, every wild cherry tree in his northern New Jersey neighborhood was under murderous attack by hordes of voracious tent caterpillars.

Hermann knew about psionics and was then in touch with Hieronymus. The Florida inventor was visiting Brig. Gen. Henry R. Gross's Homeotronic Research Foundation at the latter's farm near Harrisburg, Pa. Gross, who was then State Director of Selective Service, was working with psionic devices, and was successfully exterminating insects from great distances on more than 90 farms in the Cumberland Valley.

"Send me a photograph of your tree," Hieronymus wrote Hermann. "Put some leaves and a few caterpillars in a box and mail them along. *And don't forget to include the negative,*" he added.

This seemed a bit odd to Hermann, but he complied. Three hundred miles separated his home from the Gross farm. But in a few days, as he pulled into his driveway after work, he hit the brakes and stared in wide-eyed astonishment. Seemingly everywhere he looked, thousands of caterpillars were scurrying away from the tree. A carpet of dead insects lay in a full circle under the branches and leaves from which they'd fallen—killed by some mysterious kind of energy.

"For your records," Hermann wrote to Hieronymus later, "I think you should know that whatever you did to the cherry tree on our lawn was good. We don't have a caterpillar in sight! This isn't normal; last year we were still burning off caterpillars in late June and early July with flaming kerosene torches . . . something definite and specific was done here . . ."

Over the years individual and widely separated researchers in psionics have been discovering and rediscovering that all matter emits radiations. Mesmer's experiments goaded von Reichenbach into studying people who exhibited ESP talent. With the help of these sensitives, von Reichenbach accumulated a wealth of data indicating the existence of something he called the Odic Force. He discovered it in crystals, in heat, light, magnets, and in living cells; he found it wherever chemical reactions were taking place.

Other scientists have found the same force being generated from the growth of living cells. They called it Mitogenic Radiation. At Columbia University three scientists, I. I. Rabi, P. Kusch and S. Millman, developed a new apparatus which conclusively proved that some kind of ray or vibrations pass between one molecule and another. They showed that each molecule, living or inert, is a small radio transmitter (and receiver) that broadcasts continuously. Their waves range over the entire electromagnetic spectrum—and *beyond*. The sheer volume of these vibrations is apparently limitless. A single molecule can give off rays of a *million* different wavelengths, but only on one frequency at a time.

When the Hieronymus machine is in operation, the Eloptic Radiation stimulates the Generic Pattern of the subject and some kind of psychic bond or link is established between the emanations of the atoms and molecules of matter and the mind of the operator. Prior to 1946 when Hieronymus (who happens to be a Fellow in the Society of Electrical Engineers) patented his invention, he had learned that any mineral or chemical compound could be identified by placing an ore sample on a tray, *concentrating* on the element he was seeking to identify, and turning a dial. When the fingers with which he was stroking a small plate on the machine "stuck," he knew the dial was tuned to the right frequency. Everything has its own "rate"; it makes no difference *who* does the tuning. If the operator is thinking about *copper*, the device will detect the presence of copper (if there is any) in the sample of ore.

As a detector, it operates in much the same way as a dowsing rod. Everyone who duplicates the experiment will obtain the same dial setting, or rate, for the vibration of copper. No other metal present in the sample will register unless the operator is thinking of it while dialing. This Odic Force, Eloptic Radiation, or whatever it is, can be caught on a photographic plate and then the detector will react to a *photograph* of the mineral specimen as well as it would to the mineral itself.

Like De la Warr's camera, the Hieronymus Machine also detects emanations from blood samples, minerals, plants, insects—anything at all—that cannot be recorded by any other known method. Moreover, as John Campbell discovered, *the device works even when disconnected from a power source*, ordinary household current.

Because all psionic devices work on the same principle, they can be used as receivers *and* transmitters. This is why physical illnesses can be positively influenced when the patient is in another town or city. All it takes is a bit of saliva on a blotter, a lock of hair, a skin scraping, a blood sample, or even a photograph.

According to present understanding of psionics, the radiations from all matter in the entire Universe can be directed along a wire like electricity, or transmitted from the subject on light waves.

At first, some experimenters seem to have more natural talent, skill, or patience than others, but to the astonishment of nearly everyone who received copies of Patent No. 2,482,773 from the U.S. Patent Office (Washington, D.C. 20025), and built the device, it worked according to Hieronymus' instructions. When John Campbell built the device and encouraged Ed Hermann to test it, the "stick" occurred at the right point on the dial every time it was used.

It's a baffling, paradoxical, and altogether incredible invention. It can't really be called a machine because it operates just as well when the power is disconnected. In this respect, it's a *tool*. The key to all psionic devices is the *Mind* of the operator, which is usually tuned to the emanations of whatever object is under analysis.

Man's first really powerful tools for helping his mental capacities were the equivalents of pencil and paper. Nearly anyone can perform impressive mental feats with them. Try adding four seven-digit numbers, for example, without them; yet it isn't the paper and pencil that does the calculating—even if you can't do it without them.

Anyone interested in other psionics devices can find the equivalent (or an improved version) of the Hieronymus machine in copies of patents from The British Patent Office, Sale Branch, St. Mary Cray, Orpington, Kent; Br5 3rd; England:

Patent No. 198,018: Instrument for Detecting and Investigating Emanations Proceeding from Substances: William Ernest Boyd.

Patent No. 235,926: Apparatus for Detecting and Investigating Emanations: William Ernest Boyd.

Patent No. 272,023: Device for Testing the Radiations Emanating from Organisms: Arno Holzheimer (Plauen, Germany)

Patent No. 663,978: Detection of Emanations from Materials and Measurement of the quantities of said Materials (British patent for the Hieronymus device, granted Jan. 2, 1952): T. Galen Hieronymus.

Patent No. 515,866: Method of and Means for obtaining Photographic Images of Living and other Objects: Ruth Drown. (Psionic camera)

Patent No. 626,396: A New or Improved Apparatus for Use in the Study and Practice of Radiesthesia: Douglas Walter Atkinson.

Patent No. 761,976: Therapeutic Apparatus (The Delawarr Camera): George Walter De la Warr.

"Psionics," declared Dr. William J. Hale when he was chief of Dow Chemical's Research Division, "is the field of human achievement *beyond science.* Only after several thousand years has science been put into some kind of reasonable order. Anyone who thinks this completely new field—as broad and deep, if not more so, than all known modern science—can be thoroughly investigated in just a few decades, is sorely deluding himself!"

He wrote a book about agricultural psionics called *Farmer Triumphant,** in which he said: "The human mind capable of modulating an energy pattern has a direct connection with *physical* forces; Universal Mind is able to manifest through an energy pattern as matter. The Hieronymus device connects a purely mental function, which we call extrasensory perception, with an image on a photographic plate. These psionic devices provide us with an extradimensional tool which is able to probe the gross material results to see what is happening a little higher up on the ladder of Causation."

The fact that a psionic machine in unscrupulous hands might enable an operator, at least theoretically, to *kill* another human being, has never been fully and/or openly dealt with by the experts for fairly obvious reasons. Yet this apparently unlimited power over life and death resides in the mind of almost anyone—including skilled operators of

*Vincent Stuart, Ltd., London, 1966.

psionic devices. The incredulity of orthodox scientists provides a safe haven for the potential psionics manipulator or killer. He can cause the death of another human and literally get away with it. It will take radical new legislation and (alas!) psionic policemen to enforce such laws before there will be any protection against the misuse of psionics.

Big Science *knows* with absolute certainty that it's "impossible" to cause any physical effect from a distance of 300 to a thousand miles with a box, a dial, and a photograph. This is one reason why the prestigious, lavishly funded National Science Foundation has long refused even to *look* at a practical demonstration of the Hieronymus Machine. The fact that the Soviet Union and other Eastern European countries are developing psionics at a rapid clip cuts no ice with government officials and bureaucrats.*

More than 20 years ago however, skilled professionals and psychics such as Eileen Garrett and Martin Ebon clearly warned that the Soviets were going all-out in their efforts to train psychics, mediums, and clairvoyants, and to develop psionic devices and their psychotronic generators. At the same time, the Pentagon pointedly turned down Hieronymus' offer to test his invention for them under control conditions. The brass was hugely interested.

When John Campbell heard about it, he sent for the patent, built his own device according to specifications, tested it repeatedly, and induced everyone who visited his home in New Jersey to experiment with it. Campbell was tough-minded and individualistic and therefore *seemed* eccentric to corporation and government personnel who represented Big Science. True, he was a bit of a science-baiter, but the big man was absolutely fair and scrupulously honest when it came to the facts. Here's what he wrote to Hieronymus on June 4, 1956:

"If you can kill insect pests by working on a photograph, and at a distance of thousands of miles—*if I accept that*—it *implies that you can kill me with such a machine, despite all I might do to hide, without my having any chance whatever of protecting myself, without my knowledge or opportunity to*

*David V. Tansley, *Radionics and the Subtle Anatomy of Man.* Health Science Press, Russington, Sussex, England, 1972.

defend against the attack. The more you prove that you *can* kill living entities at a huge distance, without any understandable linkage that could be defended—the more you prove that I am helpless to protect myself. The more you make a man know that such forces exist—the less he can feel that he lives in a world of reasonable security wherein he can, at least, have warning of attack, and prepare to meet it.

"True, you're attacking only insects; you're *helping* human beings. But the implications are there, inherently, and cannot be denied. You cannot tell me how to defend myself against such an attack; if I acknowledge the reality of those forces— I acknowledge that I am helpless, and know of no defense.

". . . I selected your machine among the many possible psionic machines available because: 1) it was patented [*Campbell was probably unaware at the time of the many others that were patented.*]; 2) the patent specifically implied a mineral-analyzer, and *the life-affecting characteristics* could be ignored; 3) it *looks* like an electronic-physical machine—it *appears* to make some sort of almost-sense at the purely physical science level.

"A man can learn only at the boundary of the known; your machine *appears* to be right on the boundary between pure electronics and psionics. Therefore, it appears as though this were a learnable-understandable device that can, with a little extension of already-understood concepts and a little study, be comprehended.

"The therapeutic and diagnostic aspects of the machine— the life-force aspects—could be totally ignored, and so physical scientists could attack the problem without stirring deep, and extremely powerful fears.

"*That machine of yours is almost pure Magic.* In the old, real and potent sense; *it casts spells, imposes death-magic; and can be used for life-magic.* It operates on the anciently known laws of Sympathetic Magic; it, like Voodoo dolls, applies the law that 'The Symbol *is* the Object, and that which is done to the Symbol occurs also to the Object.'

"That's a law, too—a real one. The primitive human tribes all over the world, from Eskimos through Hawaiians, Africans, Incas, ancient Greeks and prehistory European tribes, all independently came to the same fundamental conclusions.

If such independent peoples separately reached the same conclusions—it must be that the Laws of the Universe are, in fact, involved.

"You're scaring hell out of the people who understand what you've got. You may be using it well—but *release* it, and what *limits* it? If a magician can destroy a man tracelessly—who is safe from threat, from ransom demand, from the vengeful hate of an unjust enemy?

"You're scaring people—and they have reason for their fears, while you can name *no limits* to this powerful technique!

"When I began working on the machine, I learned that it didn't need a power supply. Then I learned that it wouldn't work if a tube was missing or defective. I saw some of the other psionic machines and saw that they worked, despite the fact that their wiring system made absolutely no logical sense. From that, I derived a new concept, a theory, and made a crucial experiment.

"I have a model of your analytical machine, simplified and streamlined to the ultimate. It consists *solely of the circuit diagram;* I have a *symbol* of the prism, not a real prism, mounted on a National Velvet Vernier dial; that, and a small copper loop, alone appear on the front surface of the panel. *Back of the panel, the circuit diagram is drawn in India ink on standard drafting paper; the prism-symbol rotates in its appropriate place in the circuit diagram.* The spiral coil is drawn in India ink on paper glued to the back of the panel; it is connected with the symbolized vacuum tube cathode by a second nylon thread from my wife's sewing kit.

"The machine works beautifully; the consistency of performance is excellent.

"We're working with Magic—and Magic doesn't depend on matter, but on *form*—on *pattern* rather than substance.

"Your electronic circuit represents a pattern of relationships; this is important. The electrical characteristics are utterly unimportant, and can be dropped out completely. The machine fails when a tube burns out because that alters the pattern; it works when there is no power because the relationship of patterns is intact. My symbolic diagram works because the pattern is present . . .

"... If you can *do* at a distance through barriers—it is implicit that you could *observe* at a distance through barriers. Clairvoyance means the end of personal privacy. The fact is implicit in the action at a distance without mechanism at the other end.

"It's frightening!"

When Hieronymus filed the patent application for his device in the U.S. in 1946, he was acutely aware of its potentialities. It could be used for great good—or terrible evil. This, he explained later, was why he *deliberately* omitted some critical factors. "Those were crucial times," he said. "There was a realignment of political and military power after World War II, and I was afraid it might get into the wrong hands."

Whatever the extent of his knowledge then, Hieronymus may have used psionics to discover that the Soviet Union was even then pursuing serious, state-supported research in the practical use of parapsychology as a tool for ESPionage on an unheard-of scale. He's still noncommittal about it, but did admit it was a tough decision to make. In light of what we now know of Russia's research in parapsychology, this might be the understatement of the century.

He knew that once his device became publicly known, sooner or later somebody was sure to realize that unlimited power might be available. There are enough intelligent, clever, often cunning and unprincipled individuals (and nations) who wouldn't hesitate to use his invention for personal gain or power—at everyone's expense.

Despite these great dangers, an unusually quiet cooperation seems to exist among the working psionics experimenters in the United States and Europe. It's a kind of underground "reservoir" of physicists, biochemists, engineers, skilled technicians, and science-oriented laymen, most of whom have expressed a fear of Soviet domination of their field.

"We've never found anything we couldn't analyze chemically or otherwise," Hieronymus said. "Distance is a negligible factor, too. When we analyze our physical world we find practically *nothing* physical, just the manifestation of *energy*.

By the same means, Professor S. W. Tromp described radionics in his book *Psychical Physics:* "With an instrument, the etheric energy pattern that corresponds to any given object, substance or condition can be artificially stimulated. The process is not on the physical level. It lies beyond the limits of the five known senses and seems to be outside the measurable electromagnetic spectrum."

Psionics, by any definition, bends the mind and shatters all preconceived notions and precedents. In order to publish a 22-page statement of "Vitality Intensity Values" of the Apollo astronauts—from liftoff to splashdown, and through the quarantine periods—Hieronymus and his colleagues established the Advanced Sciences Research and Development Corporation, Inc. (T. G. Hieronymus, Director, P.O. Box 23620, Fort Lauderdale, Florida 33307)

"Of all the data collected and information covered by us during the flights," Hieronymus said, "the most important and startling is that *there is a lethal belt of radiation on the Moon,* apparently extending from about 65 miles down to approximately 15 feet from the surface . . .

"There was a noticeable drop in the general vitality (of the astronauts) and an increase in carcinogenic readings. The pathologies increased until the men actually stepped onto the Moon, then everything reversed. This situation was the same in all other lunar landings."

Hieronymus issued 500 copies of this report to interested medical men and scientists. "Eloptic Energy," he insists, "does not relate in any way to Alpha or Beta particles or to gamma rays. It doesn't fit into any part of the electromagnetic spectrum. It operates in an entirely *different* media."

The healing powers of the mind over the body are well documented—as are its negative, destructive abilities. If we have this capacity to control our *own* health and disease conditions—including that of life and death—the logical extension would be that *some* of us should also be able to exercise control over *others*. If it *can* be done, it almost certainly *is* being done! But without using psionic devices, it is almost impossible to determine how sophisticated or powerful a stage the evolution of psionics has reached during the past two decades.

Five psionics investigators have met untimely, mysterious deaths in recent years. Three of these were declared "natural" and two were listed as "suicides." To date, there's no such thing as a psionic "shield," and even if there were, it would have to be operating 24 hours a day, 365 days a year. Bell Laboratories and other electronics corporations are bidding for the rights to produce the Hieronymus device for commercial purposes.

But before these things are mass produced, we ought to learn a lot more about the strange similarities among the deaths of psionics inventors and researchers. Dr. Morris K. Jessup was listed as a suicide when he was found dead in his station wagon in Dade County Park, Fla. on the evening of April 29, 1959. Ruth Drown died in prison and three others, one a physicist, came close to almost complete understanding of psionic powers. Before his death, the physicist, who was also an astronomer, analyzed incoming light from nearby planets and distant stars by connecting a psionic device to his telescope. He reported that life exists on two planets (*other* than the earth) within our solar system. One is Venus, but Venusian life forms, according to his description, are unlike anything we know. He detected Mitogenic Radiation resulting from the growth of living cells—"the cell division in the roots of extremely large plants," he claims.

Other researchers have analyzed emanations from relics of the past. In this respect, all psionic devices, including the Hieronymus Machine, are also *time machines*. With a Delawarr adaptation, radiations from the fossils of prehistoric creatures that existed millions of years ago have been caught on film and developed.

With blood samples taken from his wife and himself, George de la Warr once turned his camera and concentrated on their wedding day, an event that had taken place nearly 30 years previously. The picture was developed before skeptical witnesses and was *recognizably* that of a young couple in somewhat outdated wedding outfits. He used this same photograph for "positive" identification that the couple were in fact himself and Mrs. de la Warr.

Psionics seems to shrink time and distance to pure illusion. Among practitioners of radionics and psionics, the eighteenth-century concept of the interplanetary ether has gained over astronomy's theory of a "dead vacuum" to explain the properties of empty space. It is from this ether, claim psionics experts, that all life and consciousness comes into material existence—and to which it returns (in a higher or more refined vibrational state) after physical "death."

In this respect, psionics holds some hope that the Universe is not a chaotic, random state of affairs. It also throws another, excitingly different kind of light on the anciently known concepts of karma and reincarnation.

As Nikola Tesla once remarked, "When science begins the study of non-physical phenomena, it will make more progress *in one decade* than in all the centuries of its existence."

That decade appears to be upon us now.

Chapter Five

The Fantastic Fields
of Life

Your body and mine are enveloped in electrodynamic fields that can be detected and measured. According to its polarity, this ambient field can predict heart disease, cancer, and a host of different diseases and ailments—*long before the appearance of physical symptoms*. Scientists who study the L-field in seeds are able to predict the size, growth patterns, and general vitality of the future plants.

These fields are related to the "aura" surrounding all biological organisms. But they are composed of such refined energies that no one believed they existed until technology enabled us to see them. Most important, these fields are influenced by the power of the human mind. "Ever since I can remember," said Edgar Cayce, the famed psychic of Virginia Beach, Va., "I have seen colors in connection with people. I don't remember when the people I met didn't register on my retina with blues, greens and reds emanating from their heads and shoulders. It was a long time before I realized that other people didn't see these colors . . ."

Cayce could have been describing the energy fields discovered by Drs. Harold S. Burr and Leonard Ravitz at Yale University's School of Medicine. Like polygraph expert Cleve Backster who in 1966 discovered something he calls "primary perception" in plants, these medical men published numerous reports describing the existence of a complex field of energy surrounding every man, woman and child and every living thing on Earth.

They call it the L-field or Field or Life—a refined form of energy which could be a kind of "higher octave" force existing beyond the familiar electromagnetic spectrum. These fields surround every cell and seed. Apparently in existence everywhere in the universe, *they coalesce prior to the formation of the physical organism* (and may survive its dissolution).

What kind of energy might exist beyond the known spectrum? One possibility is a form of radiation that exceeds the speed of light. Physicists have created a mathematical model of such a particle which, according to Einstein's general field theory, was only recently regarded as an impossibility.

Yet the scientists in search of these mysterious particles have found solutions that permit their existence—theoretically—provided that they never drop *below* light speed. They're called "tachyons" and may help to explain the "something extra" now being discovered to surround every living organism.

"Every living thing on this planet," said Dr. Burr, "from man to mice—from seeds to trees—are moulded and controlled by electrodynamic fields which can be measured with a good modern voltmeter."

This nonphysical "matrix" is the energy or force which determines the body's form and its function. It was proven by a dramatic 18-month study of women's L-fields at New York's Bellevue Hospital. With it, cervical and other types of cancer can be detected before there is any visible symptom or other manifestation of the disease.

Measurements of these L-field voltages are being used by some doctors to reveal both physical *and* mental abnormalities long before they manifest. Serious illness can now be diagnosed *before* a patient develops physical symptoms. These voltmeter diagnostic techniques fairly boggle the orthodox imagination.

"These fields of Life or L-fields," Dr. Burr said, "are now known as the basic blueprints of all life on this planet; their discovery has enormous significance for all of us. Life is no accident after all. In fact the Universe we're beginning to see is a profoundly meaningful and ordered system—*and so are we!*"

In 1966 a polygraph (lie detector) expert discovered that all life forms have a kind of "primary perception"—it is found in plants, fish, crustaceans, even tiny cells and microorganisms. And humans. Plants are able to detect human and other L-fields. Even before Cleve Backster stumbled on his now-famous laboratory discovery, a West Coast minister, the Reverend Franklin Loehr, reported that two boxes in which he had placed identical amounts of seed and soil had—*through the power of human thought*—produced completely different results.

Dr. Loehr wanted to prove to his congregation that prayer is very real and very effective. The care and conditions given to each box of seed and soil were identical. The only variable was that Dr. Loehr's parishioners prayed for the seedlings in one box and ignored (or in some cases, actually "cursed") those in the other.

To everyone's amazement the prayed-over seeds blossomed many times faster and produced sturdy, beautiful flowers. The seeds in the other box managed to produce a few yellowish, stunted growths. Obviously, "prayer" has some kind of power, but how is the mind linked to such energy? What is it?

Researchers have found that biological fields can be detected in the air surrounding every living organism. These fields are intimately related to human emotional and mental processes. The spectacular technique for photographing the energy *patterns* of L-fields was discovered in England years before the celebrated discovery of Kirlian photography in the Soviet Union.

The Delawarr camera is based on some of the same principles as the Hieronymus Machine. One of the most important and startling of the thousands of experiments in radionic (or "psionic") photography was made in England in 1958, and demonstrates the potency of the L-field. De la Warr used his patented camera to photograph a sample of ordinary tap water at Oxford. The resulting picture showed seven thin bright lights of varying lengths radiating from their common center point.

It wasn't at all unusual. Every substance photographed with the Delawarr camera had its own characteristic radiation pattern. But then they asked a priest, the Rev. P. W. Eardsley, to bless the water before they took another picture of the same sample.

"Something" completely unexplainable (by all scientific

means) happened: a totally *different* radiation pattern appeared in the photograph—this time *a brilliant cross!*

"It must always be borne in mind," wrote British attorney John Wilcox in his book,* "that whatever it is that is being photographed, it is NOT the object itself, that is to say, not the physical or material aspect of it which is all that is perceptible to the physical senses. Objects have residing in them or associated with them qualities and conditions appertaining to their primary or fourth-dimensional states, the presence of which cannot be detected through the agency of the five senses."

Totally independently of each other, experimenters are making parallel discoveries. In Cleve Backster's New York City laboratory in 1966, for example, when he was checking out some polygraph equipment, he wondered whether it could measure the rate at which water rose from the roots of his office philodendron plants to its leaves.

Backster clipped a couple of polygraph electrodes to the leaves, then watered the plant. Within minutes, he noticed an "unusual tracing—similar to a reaction pattern of a human being under strong emotional stimulation."

Backster's eyes were riveted to the swinging needle of his machine. "I was absolutely entranced," he said. "I *still* didn't have any idea of what caused the initial reaction. I wasn't thinking of causing anything to happen or of harming the plant." But that's when he got the idea of burning the leaf with a match to see if there'd be another reaction.

"At the very instant I made that decision," he said later, "there was a dramatic and prolonged upward sweep in the tracing. I had not moved or touched the plant." (In a human being, a tracing like this would indicate "fear.")

Since that milestone discovery Backster and his associates have accumulated a wealth of new evidence. Their previous notions were shattered—not only do plants "feel," they also seem capable of reading people's minds. When James Collier, a skeptical writer for the Sunday edition of the Balitimore *Sun* came to New York to check the philodendron story he swore that one of Backster's plants actually caught him in a

*Radiations: Theory and Practice, Robert Jenkins, Ltd., 3 Duke of York Street, London S.W., 1960.

lie! It was that plant that was rigged to the lie detector, *not* Collier!

To eliminate unconscious interference—or the possibility of human error—Backster and an associate, Robert Henson, set up an elaborate double-blind electronic feedback system in which living shrimp were randomly dumped into boiling water by remote control. They had no way of knowing in which rooms the shrimp were being boiled to death; their only clues were readings from the plants that were hooked to polygraph machines in each room.

When the shrimp were dumped into boiling water the polygraph registered an enormous flurry of energy from the plant in the room where the automatic equipment had tossed the marine animals to their doom.

"Can it be that when cell life dies," Backster wondered, "it broadcasts a signal to *other* living cells?" Apparently it can and does. But nobody knows why such a mechanism exists.

Since then, Backster and his colleagues have widened their investigations to include all kinds of fruit and vegetables and yeasts and mold cultures—also blood specimens and scrapings from the roof of a human mouth. They extended these observations into the realm of amoebae, paramecia, and even spermatazoa—all of which supported their belief that "primary perception" is a fantastic universal phenomenon. They had detected a previously unknown communication signal that links all living things. (In 1971 a California scientist accidentally recorded similar signals with a sophisticated array of electronic and psionic equipment. *These* signals however, came from outer space! (See Chapter 11, "Contact!".)

"We know the signal is somewhere beyond the known frequencies such as AM, FM, or any kind of signal which we can shield by ordinary means," said Backster. "Even distance doesn't seem to impose any limitation. I've tried shielding the plants with a Faraday screen cage (to stop electrical penetration) and even lead-lined containers. *The signal doesn't seem to fall within any known portion of the electromagnetic spectrum.*"

Backster converts these biological signals to an electrical current that can be measured by the polygraph. The most successful or "green thumb" gardeners believe that plants have an affinity to the people who feed and care for them. Plants, trees, and other organisms generate or are encased in their own electrodynamic fields. These "energy bodies" are sensitive and responsive to the human L-field (and possibly vice-versa).

This is a prodigious manifestation that supports the evidence of the power of human thought, or telepathy, the T-field. As Dr. Banesh Hoffmann, one of Albert Einstein's assistants, said in a joint statement with the Nobel Prize-winning physicist, Pascal Jordan, "A gravitational field has some similarity with the force with transmits *telepathic* information, in that both act at a distance and penetrate all obstacles."

Thought therefore, is a product of the mind which in turn influences or controls the L-field. In a scientific paper that is now famous in its field, "Electrocyclic Phenomena and Emotional States," Dr. Leonard Ravitz reported that "voltage measurements of the L-field can be used to diagnose the conditions not only of the body, but also *of the mind.* L-field voltage changes reflect subjective conditions such as schizophrenia and even the depth of an hypnotic trance."

Some parapsychologists believe that the T-field, or conscious thought, is "totally independent of the physical brain." It may even be another kind of field altogether. In fact, Dr. Harold S. Burr's medical research at Yale University's School of Medicine has developed into an almost metaphysical picture of man as an interactive and purposeful element in the Universe.

When California physicist L. George Lawrence recorded the first "biological" signals from outer space on October 29, 1971, they seemed so purposefully generated and regularly cycled that Lawrence concluded that they were of intelligent origin.

If so, the L-field recording needed coherent mental energy and highly sophisticated direction to make the transmissions. Carl Gustav Jung, the famed psychiatrist who also investigated astrology, meditation, Zen Buddhism, and even alchemical imagery, said before his death in 1960 that "The frontier of the human mind is moving closer and closer to the portcullis of God."

The equally illustrious Jesuit anthropologist and paleontologist, Pierre Teilhard de Chardin, sensed the growing awareness of the Universal L-field—a kind of Collective Human Biosphere.

"The mechanism of biological evolution," he said, "gives place to the special forces released by the psychic phenomenon of humanity ... right before our eyes there is a *growing biological entity such as has never before existed on Earth*— the growth, *outside* and *above* the biosphere of an added planetary layer, an envelope of thinking substance to which, for the sake of convenience and symmetry, I have given the name of the *Noosphere.*"

(By definition, this is another name for the T-field, or *the T-field of the Mass Human Consciousness.*)

Brain expert Dr. Wilder Penfield and the Soviet Union's Professor Leonid Vasiliev have independently discovered that these fields regulate and control every living thing. In his book, *Blueprint for Immortality*, Dr. Burr reported that "although they are infinitely complicated, L-fields—like other electromagnetic fields—are influenced by the greater fields of the Universe. Man, therefore, is an integral part of the Universe and shares in its purpose and destiny."

An intriguing notion that keeps recurring from the dimmest days of prehistory is that Homo sapiens has certain characteristics in common with animals, birds, fish, and even plants. Charles Darwin once observed that "plants have sense organs and some sort of nervous system." We now have scientific evidence of it.

In the past few years Cleve Backster has demonstrated experimentally that all forms of life—down to the simplest cells—are indeed influenced by the human mind. Plants sense human emotion and even respond to whatever people are thinking.

"Once a plant is accustomed to you," says Backster, "you can be anywhere and it can tune in as if nothing separated it from you." He is now investigating plant "memory" and the equally interesting phenomenon of "feeling" in eggs. His experiments agree with Dr. Burr's discovery that the Fields of Life exist and are detectable *long before there is any evidence of physical life.*

Backster had a laboratory watchdog, a Doberman pin-scher, and added raw eggs to the animal's chow "to make his coat glossier." Once when he cracked an egg in the lab, he noticed that a plant which happened to be connected to a polygraph machine gave off a particularly strong reaction. He examined the strip tracing and repeated the experiment. There was another strong reaction from the plant.

He wondered what would happen if he attached an egg directly to the polygraph machine. Instead of cracking it, he taped electrodes to each end of the egg. To his complete amazement, the recording revealed a cycle frequency of 170 beats a minute—roughly *the heartbeat rate for the embryo of a chicken!*

He didn't think it could be possible, so he cracked the egg in a bowl and saw that it was completely fresh. There was no embryo, no trace of a nervous or circulatory system. In fact, the egg wasn't even fertilized! Nothing physical could account for the recording. This was strong evidence for the existence of the manifestation of what some physicists call "continuous vector fields of force."

Although L-fields appear to be unrelated to magnetic fields, they are nevertheless characterized by *intensity* and *polarity*, i.e., strength and direction of rotation. These factors are typical of both atoms and entire solar systems.

Biological fields can be detected in the air surrounding every living organism. There are fields within fields within fields. Their cycles of flux and reflux reflect what is called "the momentum of living matter in time." From the tiniest cell to the largest creatures on Earth, the electrocyclic timing of every living thing mirrors the larger cycles of the L-field. Each L-field, in turn, is attuned to the global and interplanetary magnetic fields, a fact that should be of enormous interest to astrologers who are scientifically inclined.

At the Fifth International Congress for Hypnosis and Psychosomatic Medicine, held in Germany in 1972, L-field expert Dr. Ravitz reported, "Electric fields control birth, growth and death as well as the maintenance and repair of all living things. These L-fields are *different* from the alternating-current output of the brain and heart as well as from the epiphenomenal skin resistance. Rather, *they serve as an electronic matrix to keep the corporeal form in shape."*

It's the L-field that supervises the renewal of the cellular structure of the human body every few years. It's the L-field, NOT the DNA molecule, Dr. Ravitz pointed out, which molds the new material into the same design as the old. "This explains why, even though you might not see a friend for a year or more, during which time all the molecules of his face and head have completely changed, he is recognizably the same."

It also helps to explain the mystery of memory. You can remember events 5, 10, or even 20 years ago even though every molecule of your brain has been replaced—perhaps as many as half a hundred times.

In the exciting experiments at Yale University's School of Medicine, Dr. Burr, Dr. F. S. C. Northrum, and Dr. E. K. Hunt mapped out and proved the existence of the L-field with high input impedance, i.e., highly sensitive voltmeters which did *not* draw current from the organisms being studied. In this way they succeeded in measuring pure voltage differences in various parts of the L-field *without interfering with it in any way.*

"The L-field proved to be the controlling force, and could forecast the future conditions of the form it controlled. For example, a study of the L-fields of seeds predicted the growth patterns, sizes and general vitality of the future plants," said Dr. Ravitz. "Field measurements of *unfertilized* frog eggs show the head-tail axis of its future nervous system. This orientation remains the same even after fertilization takes place. Ovulation, wound-healing, peripheral nerve injury, and even cancer, all have their unique field correlates to every form of life, including human beings."

During the early tests of these electrodynamic fields, Dr. Louis Langman, an obstetrician and gynecologist with New York University's School of Medicine, discovered hundreds of instances of cervical cancer among female patients at Bellevue Hospital. The L-fields of the majority of women with nonmalignant complaints measured electro*positive* with equal consistency.

Here was an extraordinarily significant discovery, confirmed by an 18-month study of cell and tissue cultures from women admitted to Bellevue's gynecological clinic. And here is where Backster's "genesis" theory seems to have been vindicated: among women from whom voltmeter measurements of their L-fields were *negative* (and yet showed no detectable symptoms of cancer), these same women were *later* discovered to have developed malignancies of the cervix. At the time, this was the clearest possible indication that the L-field could "forecast" whatever it was "planning" to generate within the physical body! In cases where hysterectomies were performed, the L-fields of those women returned to normal electro*positive*.

"It seems pretty obvious," Dr. Langman observed, "that this technique can be extremely valuable in the early detection—or actual *avoidance*—of cancer. We could select patients with negative polarity, consider them 'suspect' and follow them with great care. There is solid evidence that cancer can now be prevented before it is 'scheduled' to occur. If so, then *any* disease, perhaps even aging, can be postponed—perhaps indefinitely."

These "higher energy bodies" of *all* living things can predict future developments, even in the organism's surrounding environment. For example, in the electrodynamic field tests of trees that have been continuously monitored since the early 1940s, electrodes that were permanently embedded in the inner (growing) layers of the trees showed regular changes that were totally unrelated to then-current environmental conditions such as temperature, humidity, air pressure, and sunlight. Yet these changes predicted in great detail events that actually occurred in the environment during the next 48 hours—barometric changes, thunderstorms, *even sunspots!* Small wonder that such discoveries boggle the imaginations of conservative scientists!

A tree's L-field can anticipate the effect of atmospheric electricity and other things (in its cambia, or inner layers) and produce a "reading" as though the tree is *currently* being stimulated.

In a human being, the L-field fluctuation means that the physical body will soon undergo specific changes and might even suffer an injury, a fact that gives it clairvoyant abilities.

L-field measurements in humans can anticipate virtually ANY future malady or malfunction—be it cancer, heart disease, arthritis, emphysema, kidney trouble—*anything*. No study of the "self-replicating" DNA molecule has ever given such a concrete evidence of predicting future illness.

Edward W. Russell, in *Design for Destiny*,* says, "In their present preoccupation with particles, biology and biochemistry are in the same stage that physics was years ago before 'particle physics' gave place to 'field physics.' When biology finally matures and 'particle biology' gives way to *'field biology'* the role of genes and DNA will be seen in its true perspective."

The wooden idols of primitive civilizations were carved by talented tribesmen; the artist is greater than his creation, therefore it has no godlike powers over him. Neither genes nor DNA molecules have any power over the organism of which it is a part. The body is far greater than the sum of its component organs, cells, and molecules. In fact the molecules are so much simpler in structure than the bodily organism as a whole that there's just no way for DNA or any other kind of molecule to control the entire organism.

Only L-fields know the organism's needs in advance, especially during growth. Only L-fields can send the right molecular substances to the necessary part of the body at the right time. The genetic theory groundlessly presupposes that DNA and genes act as matrices that somehow enable molecules and cells to "replicate" themselves. But to function at all, *a matrice* MUST *be independent of and unaffected by the material it molds,* and DNA is *not* independent of the body. Paradoxically, the L-field is, and it is *not*.

At any rate, the molecules of the body are continually breaking down, interacting, and restructuring each other. It naturally follows then, that they cannot of themselves serve as matrices. *Only L-fields can anticipate or predict* in which way an animal's nervous system will develop. Only an L-field can decide the sex of a human baby or how strong and healthy the future man or woman will be. This does seem to reduce whatever modicum of conscious control we have over

*Neville Spearman, Ltd., London, 1971.

such things, but so did being born black, white, brown, or yellow, or male or female—before L-fields were discovered.

The human L-field is different, more complex than those of trees, animals, or any other life form. In a study of 50,000 people since 1948 (at Yale, Duke University, and the University of Pennsylvania Schools of Medicine), their L-field readings yielded such subjective changes as feeling, emotion, and behavior that were beyond the detection capabilities of any other method.

Unlike the electroencephalogram of brain-wave output to measure the depth of sleep, the L-field can detect the actual depth of the hypnotic trance—something heretofore unheard of. It's a powerful but subtle force, able to detect the future development of peptic ulcers, allergies, and even confused mental conditions such as schizophrenia.

"To ignore the study of the overriding L-field in favor of some anthropomorphic gene or DNA molecule," says Edward Russell, "is unproven supposition—perhaps 'superstition' would be more accurate."*

The L-field that keeps your body in recognizable shape over a period of many years MUST not change. The cells and molecules of your body are constantly being taken apart, broken up, and rebuilt. The overriding matrix which maintains the constant pattern of this ever-changing material must be absolutely *permanent*. Your body is *not* some miraculous exception to the universal law of energy fields. These fields of energy *control* the chemistry of all cells and molecules instead of the other way around. L-fields therefore simply *can't* be influenced by them.

It seems almost beyond human comprehension at the moment, but there does seem to be some kind of eternal, universal, interflow of countless forms of energy—from the tiniest known fields within the atom to supercolossal gravitational and other fields of the planets and even stars and galaxies which exert their power over vast cosmic distances. It's conceivable that endless hierarchies of energies, some spanning the entire Universe in a single instant, exist in multidi-

Ibid.

mensional stages. The universal L-field may be but a single manifestation of these highly refined forces.

Your L-field is not generated by your body like the biomagnetic field or electroencephalographic waves produced by the brain. Instead, it *determines* the form and function of your body and is apparently indestructible. Your L-field existed before you were born and there's now strong scientific evidence suggesting that it survives the cessation of the body's physical functioning. It is, in fact, the body's motivating energy and is intimately associated with individual consciousness—your essential identity, your true self, or—if you prefer—your immortal *soul*.

Your nervous system, for example, did not develop entirely because generations of humans adapted to a hostile terrestrial environment. New discoveries in radionics and psionics indicate that it came into being as a direct result of dynamic forces *superimposed* on groups of physical cells by your field pattern. Your personal L-field and T-field may either be interchangeable or some kind of dual manifestation of the same refined energy.

The indestructible quality of L-fields suggests that 1) they are changeless, and 2) they are therefore not subject to what is known as physical evolution. It's possible that there's another area of "Being," a different state or "dimension" where the Universe exists in a kind of "Eternal Now"—a "timeless" condition. This suggests that our conception of time—even our experience in it—may be nothing at all like our subjective sense of it.

Let's suppose there's a two-dimensional or flat Universe. Creatures living in this flatland would find it *extremely* difficult to visualize what "up" or "down" means. A three-dimensional sphere entering a two-dimensional world could only be perceived as a circle, if a small enough segment were inserted. Our conception of time may be equally limited. We can use an example here: a pilot flying overhead, say, sees what the motorist below him sees. But he has the advantage of a higher perspective and can see where the motorist *has* been—and where he *will* be in five minutes—*at the same time*.

If our conception of "past" and "future" are equally subjective, they could very well coexist with the present. Because L-fields are changeless they appear to exist in a different dimension, rate of vibration or state where all time is "Now."

But Drs. Burr, Ravitz, Northrup, and others are not suggesting that the L-field is the same as the traditional *soul*, although it shares some of the same characteristics. Psychics such as Edgar Cayce can "see" the L-field as an aura of streaming colors surrounding the human body—or any other living organism. In the Soviet Union the development of the Kirlian camera enables scientists to photograph the human electrodynamic field—*in color motion pictures!*

Monitoring the L-field by doctors on a regular basis promises to provide the most foolproof early warning system for all diseases to which human beings are prone. As Dr. Leonard Ravitz reported in the *Journal of the American Society of Psychosomatic Dentistry and Medicine*, "Living matter and even Mind itself can now be understood as based on relativity field physics through which we can now detect a measurable property of total state function ... even hypnosis can be regarded as a natural field phenomenon, independent of any 'hypnotist.' It happens naturally when you concentrate. Hypnosis, health, disease and aging," he added, "have been measured in terms of changing intensities and directions of natural L-field energy, an approach fusing the time factor, or electrocyclic phenomena of all living things."

And here's what Dr. F. L. Kunz said about the Electrodynamic Theory of Life in his *Main Currents in Modern Thought*: "We are close to the kind of breakthrough in biologic sciences which has brought the physical sciences to their present degree of control and refinement. The implications for education, and indeed for all socio-cultural aspects of human life, are without precedent."

There's definitely something "behind" all this. It isn't for nothing that these breakthroughs are occurring at this precise time in history. That "something" could be such an explosion of increased awareness, a mass raising of species consciousness to prepare us for a revolutionary advance almost beyond present human understanding—something that, if it happened prematurely, might be too shocking for all of us to contemplate at once.

Try to imagine the reaction of the Puritans in early New England if they could have been shown some of today's hard-core cinematic pornography and surrealistic violence!

Right now it's all but impossible to realize what it would mean to put biology and psychology on an equal basis, say, to mathematics and physics. Dr. Kunz's statement implies that although the L-field controls every facet of health, aging, and mental well-being, the Mind is capable of exercising almost total control of the L-field. Something like this has been the accomplished objective of mystics of the East for centuries. There is now reason to believe that in some dimly remote ancient time it was regularly and successfully practiced.

A young California radiation therapist gave a dramatic demonstration that we all have this power to a certain degree—and that it can be trained and developed, just as the yogis have always claimed. Dr. Carl Simonton succeeded in helping terminally ill cancer patients to cure themselves through *meditation*.

"Mind plays a much bigger part in healing than anyone has been willing to admit. It's not exactly the sort of thing you learn in medical school," he said with a broad grin, "but it certainly works and that's all that's important."

Simonton represents a new, practical breed of doctor. He's head of the radiation therapy department of Travis Air Base Hospital, and recently published a scientifically documented report on 50 cancer patients who were asked to "help themselves by putting their minds to work applying 'thought power' to their problem."

His first patient, for example, had an extensive tumor of the throat. "I asked him to make a mental picture of the disease, the way *he* saw it and understood it," Simonton reported. "Then I asked him to visualize his own body defenses at work."

The therapist began this line of inquiry by wondering just why two to five percent of so-called "incurable" cancer patients managed to survive. "I found that in 100 percent of those cases the patient had a strong will to live. My problem then was to instill the same attitude in the rest of my patients." Dr. Simonton now uses meditation with three-quarters of his terminally ill cancer cases.

Cleve Backster's discoveries of the heartbeat of an embryo chick in a fresh, unfertilized egg and of the symbiotic relationship between plants and people have also convinced him that we "tell" our L-fields whether we desire a strong, healthy, disease-free body or a weak, sickly one. *"If our negative thoughts and emotions can damage or kill plants and other living things at a distance* OUTSIDE *our bodies, it's easy to imagine the damage done by such thoughts and emotions within,"* he said. *"Our minds can control the L-field—the energy blueprint around which new matter coalesces to form the organic structures of our bodies."*

Call it the "idea" of the condition of every physical organ in your body—it exists as part of your L-field and *precedes* the development of that condition (whatever it may be) by months, even *years!* In one sense this makes *us* almost totally responsible for our own continual creation. The hard fact is that all of us become, in varying degrees, pretty much whatever we think about with strong emotion most of the time. If this were *not* so, it would be impossible for cancer patients who are terminally ill and ready to die to cure themselves through positive meditation.

Where does the L-field come from? How is it generated? What are its boundaries in time and space? Unfortunately, we have no clearly defined answers to such questions yet. It may be that they are eternal—or, that they came into existence when the Universe was created—*or both*. In any event, at the present stage of L-field research such questions pose fantastic philosophical as well as scientific problems. It isn't necessary to understand psionics thoroughly in order to use it constructively. Electricity and magnetism are "incompletely understood."

Not only is the discovery of this new kind of energy one of the most hopeful signs for the future of humanity, it's also the beginning of a bridge between physics and parapsychology, or medicine and biomagnetic healing.

The interesting fact is that there's now about 50 years of compelling evidence that human beings are much more than skin, muscle, bone, and blood. Fifty years, coincidentally, is just about the same period that has elapsed since the discoveries of radio waves and other radiations, new uses for electromagnetic fields and the birth of an electronic technology which is now employed in the development of supersophisticated psionic machines. None of this, it seems to me, is pure "coincidence." There is more and more reason to believe that the use of lodestones and magnets by ancient physicians in healing was an attempt to piece together the surviving remnants of a once-mighty system of advanced electromagnetic technology.

Because—in Real Universe terms—*it works.* If we're just beginning to rediscover the beneficial effects of magnetism, imagine what was known and practiced one hundred thousand years ago!

Chapter Six

The Miracle of
Biomagnetic Healing

The late, much-loved Roberto Clemente was one of Puerto Rico's many major-league baseball players who was treated and rapidly healed by the biomagnetic treatments of that island's Ralph V. Sierra.

Dr. Sierra is a dynamic, irrepressibly warm and friendly chiropractor who has also kept Orlando Cepeda's torn and twisted ligaments and kneecap healing through grueling games with magnetic bandages of his own design. Sierra, who is in his 70s, but who looks and acts like he's 40 or so, works closely with the island commonwealth's other doctors and hospitals. In fact, they often send patients to his modest research laboratory for treatment.

He is one of those researchers who independently discovered that the relationship between electricity and magnetism has a remarkable similarity to that which exists between human telepathic or psychic ability and *gravity*.

On the face of it, that may seem astounding, but in view of what we've learned about biorhythm, economic cycles, cosmic rhythms, and human responses to electrical and magnetic fields, the latest cure for cancer for example, might be as simple as exposure to a magnetic field or even breathing negatively charged ions. With weak electrical currents, severe wounds and broken bones are being healed three to five times as fast as the body's normal regenerating processes permit.

Halting the ravages of age and regrowing amputated arms and legs with small electrical charges may seem like fantasy or science fiction now, but such miracles are on the way. The arresting of aging and the regrowth of lost limbs has already been partially successful on laboratory test animals.

In one way or another nearly every human ailment is affected by electromagnetism—both cosmic and terrestrial. Until the recent discovery of the strange reactions of wildlife to what is now called "electromagnetic pollution," there were no known adverse side effects from exposure to magnetic fields, regardless of their strength or intensity. This was mainly the "waste" from the energy that runs our complex civilization—electrical power lines, radio and television transmitters, even mircrowave ovens.

Conversely, any living thing deprived of the Earth's relatively weak magnetic field for prolonged periods will suffer complex, distressing illness—*and will eventually die*. Every known mass extinction of earthly life—including the dinosaurs—occurred when the planet's magnetic field was reversed. When this happens there are periods of zero magnetism which, if prolonged, can kill every living thing in the null geomagnetic area.

The primary discovery of the human biomagnetic field was made when Dr. Robert O. Becker of New York's Upstate Medical Center mapped it out during his researches in Syracuse. During one after another series of highly specialized experiments, the evidence compiled by Dr. Becker and his colleagues (Dr. Charles Bachman and Professor Howard Friedman) persistently implied that magnetism was in fact the very *key* to the secret of life! It is a nonphysical force that affects all living organisms.

Becker is the guiding genius behind the first widely announced success of biomagnetic healing. A team of surgeons at the University of Pennsylvania Medical School vindicated Becker with the first recorded electromagnetic healing of a serious fracture. A 51-year-old woman suffered a cracked ankle bone that became infected and refused to heal for over two years. Under a contract from the Office of Naval Research, the medical school developed a small skin-implanted power pack which effectively resolved the problem of delivering a constant current to the bone in spite of steadily increasing tissue resistance.

The team, headed by Drs. Carl Brighton and Zachary Friedenberg, inserted the negative pole of the circuit (the cathode) at the point of the fracture; the anode was taped to the skin nearby. A small cast was wrapped around her ankle and the power source—a small battery pack about the size of a penny, with resistors and field effect transistors—was taped to the cast. This pack supplied a constant 10-microampere current to the fracture area 24 hours a day for nine weeks until X rays showed that the break was fully healed. The technique is now being widely studied and used on the other patients with fractures that stubbornly refuse to heal on schedule.

Becker and his colleagues have long known that the biomagnetic field at the front of the brain is negative, and that it is positive at the back of the brain centering on the brain stem leading to the central nervous system. During early experiments, he found that by suddenly reversing this polarity in test animals they were rendered effectively and immediately unconscious. By some roundabout logic this led to the conclusion that by enhancing the natural bioelectrical field, the healing of open wounds and broken bones could be enormously speeded up.

Such weird and wonderful results attributed to the effects of magnetism on the human body have intrigued man since ancient times. As a general rule, however, doctors seem to put down the most interesting claims made for electromagnetic therapy.

According to a spokesman for the American Medical Association, "Thousands of sick people could be victimized by false hopes raised by stories of miracle cures. It's still a very new field."

Before he founded the Institute of Biomagnetics, New York's Dr. Kenneth S. MacLean spent many years exposing experimental animals to varying intensities of magnetism generated by heavy-duty electrical coils. He experimented on himself by spending hundreds of hours working (and even sleeping) in a 3600-gauss magnetic field. Afterward, MacLean cautiously began to accept cancer patients considered to be "hopeless" by other doctors. He exposed these terminal sufferers to an average of 10 magnetic treatments apiece. By carefully studying their microscopic cellular changes under strict laboratory control conditions, he concluded that exposure to strong magnetic fields was at least beneficial in every case and harmful in none. His patients reacted so favorably—in some cases becoming totally pain free—that he was encouraged to expand his electromagnetic treatments.

It was among the elderly that he first noticed a strange "rejuvenating" effect that coincided with prolonged exposure to his artificially created magnetic fields. After 10 half-hour sessions under the "electromagnetic activator," some of his patients' white hair showed a definite darkening. (Under a microscope, each "white" hair is actually transparent—something like a glass tube.) In some unknown way, magnetism was either reactivating or restoring the melanin (pigmentation) of their hair.

"There were additional signs of regained health," MacLean said. "At first I couldn't bring myself to believe that so many of these malignancies were actually regressing." He displayed scores of "before and after" color slides of microscopic tissue cultures taken from his patients. (MacLean is a physician specializing in gynecology and cytology.) In a significant number of cases, the slides indicated a definite regression of wild cellular growth after prolonged electromagnetic treatment. It was extremely unlikely that they could all be attributed to what doctors refer to as "spontaneous regression." This unexplainable return to normalcy is observed in only a tiny percentage of advanced cancer cases.

MacLean's subdued enthusiasm occasionally broke through his professional attitude. "I can't say anything officially yet," he confessed, "but hell—let's face it—this treatment is a godsend. It's good for almost *anything!*"

At the Environmental Psychophysiology Laboratory of Laurentian University in Ontario, Canada, Dr. M.A. Persinger has set up the first international forum dealing with biomagnetic healing, terrestrial and cosmic influences on human beings. "We're primarily concerned with the effects of extremely low frequency electric, magnetic and sonic fields," he said, "but the importance of geomagnetism, seismic stresses and planetary influences on human behavior and health can't be overemphasized. This includes verbal behavior concerning putative 'parapsychological events.' "

In certain respects oxygen is magnetic and holds positive or negative charges. Although they probably knew nothing about negative ionization, intelligent observers have known for centuries that changes in human behavior were somehow related to subtle alterations in the atmosphere—the air we breathe.

Some of these changes occur in 27½-day lunar synodic cycles. Sweden's Nobel Prize-winning chemist, Svante Arrhenius, proved that the ion conductivity in the atmosphere coincided with a sharp upswing of crime every 27½ days.

The Foehn was once called a "Wind of Evil" in Switzerland. This warm, dry current of air always coincides with extreme restlessness and a radical increase in the amount of violent—often downright senseless—crimes. Another wind like this blows from the Libyan desert and is usually accompanied by extremely unpleasant changes in human personality and behavior, during which crimes of violence and passion run rampant. All along the northern Mediterranean, judges recognize the connection of this Sirocco with these changes in human behavior. Enlightened judges usually impose very light sentences on people who commit uncharacteristic crimes during these periods.

When the air is powerfully charged with positive ionization, many people *do* act irresponsibly. The American Institute of Medical Climatology in Philadelphia made practical use of the fact that *negatively* ionized air is physically and emotionally beneficial to about 65 percent of the population. The other 35 percent seems to experience adverse reactions to negatively ionized air, and vice versa.

During the A.I.M.C.'s pioneering experiments with the effects of electrical currents and magnetic fields, Dr. Igho H. Kornblueh exposed patients suffering the prolonged agony of body burns to negatively ionized air. It seemed almost miraculous that patients with third-degree burns covering 90 percent of their bodies could obtain almost complete freedom from pain simply by breathing negatively polarized ions. Moreover, the healing process was speeded up.

Negative ionization promotes a general feeling of wellbeing. The effect runs all the way from the relief of headaches and minor pain and fatigue to the alleviation of the dreadful agony of the advanced stages of cancer. Philco Corporation produced an electronic-ion-producing device patterned after Dr. Kornblueh's prototype, and called it the "Ionotron 8000."

Now negative ionization is being used to strengthen tooth enamel, to resist cavities and dental decay. The American Chemway Corporation has American and European patents for its "ionic" toothbrush. It was once believed by dental experts that the way fluoride gets into the system is that sound teeth absorb fluoride ions. A new theory is that the enamel wall is *negatively* charged and therefore acts as an "ionic sieve." It is believed to resist the penetration of negative ions and to facilitate the passage of positively charged ions. If so, the negatively charged fluoride ions *never* succeed in getting through the tooth enamel!

Chemway's brush introduces ions of soluble salts into the body's tissues with an electric current. Their device looks like an ordinary toothbrush with two contact pieces of different metals. One of these is fixed on the neck of the toothbrush near the handle, so that it touches the lips when the teeth are being brushed. The other contact is buried under the bristles. Toothpaste with flouride salt forms an electrolyte, and an electric current of about two volts or less is generated.

As computers become more sophisticated—some of them actually duplicating the processes of intelligent behavior by learning from their own mistakes—they've also become almost as sensitive as human brains to small electrical currents. Discharges of static electricity too small to be felt by a human can reset a computer's flip-flop switch.

People who walk across a rug can build up a charge of 5000 volts even in a relatively dry room. This voltage can be discharged into the capacitors of a computer, causing all kinds of trouble. Although you can barely feel a shock of 2500 volts (even 5000 volts isn't painful—just a noticeable tingle), electrical discharges as low as 2000 volts—too small to be felt by a human—can erase the entire memory bank of a high-speed computer. Indeed, an electrical shock will pass completely through the components of a low-speed computer in an apparent "search" for a high-speed switch to trigger.

Radar and radio transmitters can also raise havoc with computers. Airport radar at a distance of nearly a half mile recently erased the Internal Revenue's records on its computer tapes in Baltimore. Unfortunately, the IRS didn't have duplicate files, and it took more than six months to restore just a fraction of the data.

These similarities between the effects of ionization, electricity, and magnetism on machines and humans raises some rather fascinating questions. How complex will computers have to become before their malfunctions—like that of human beings—can be treated with magnetic fields?

At New York's Upstate Medical Center, research orthopedic surgeon Robert O. Becker (who also happens to be associate chief of staff for research at the Syracuse V.A. Hospital) established long ago that the biomagnetic and electrical fields of patients suffering from wounds and broken bones jumps sharply from negative (normal) to positive (traumatic). As healing progresses however, the biomagnetic field slowly returns to its normal negative state. More than 10 years ago, Dr. Becker and his colleagues were already increasing the speed of healing among test animals with negative electrical stimulation.

Becker has advanced farther and faster than anyone in his field. Because of his remarkable laboratory successes, he is convinced that the application of small amounts of negative electric current to the stumps of traumatized limbs will soon enable doctors to regenerate the arms, legs, hands, and feet of human amputees!

He was puzzled by the fact that higher animals lacked the ability of, say, a lizard to grow a tail, or a worm to regenerate the entire lower half of its body. Other creatures such as the hydra have long puzzled scientists by their strange ability to regrow amputated extremities.

Without resorting to long-range genetic engineering, Becker has regenerated the limps of animals as high on the evolutionary scale as the rat. In his early experiments on opossums and frogs, he achieved partial success in regrowing amputated limbs with slightly charged negative electric current.

During 15 years of doggedly determined work, he tried to prove that the reason man and other higher mammals cannot regenerate lost or damaged limbs is because we have somehow lost the ability to generate sufficient biomagnetic power to stimulate new limb "buds."

As far back as 1960, Becker applied magnetic fields and

electric currents to the human central nervous system and learned that changes in bodily and emotional rhythms could be reinforced—even changed. He also discovered that the organized (direct current) activity of the brain seemed to govern human behavior patterns.

Despite his outstanding success, some of his concepts are—at least by currently accepted standards—nothing less than awesome! The slender, genial scientist is considered by those who know him as a natural candidate for a Nobel Prize, yet he is roundly criticized by others because the evidence he has accumulated suggests that electromagnetic and *cosmic* forces influence biological and mental rhythms. This is widely condemned as being a scientific basis for astrology. Becker, however, couldn't care less about where the facts lead. They're *true*. He proved that the biomagnetic charge (an integral part of the system) could be influenced with external force fields (magnetic and electrostatic) as well as by changing the levels and magnetic polarization of the air we breathe.

Even Russian parapsychologists report that air ionization strongly affects human ESP abilities. People can't concentrate and often lose their psychic abilities during thunderstorms when the local geomagnetic field fluctuates wildly. This fact prompted Dr. Leonid L. Vasiliev, a physiologist and winner of the Lenin prize for his work on the effects of ionization on humans, to introduce moderately strong magnetic fields during ESP experiments. "We surround both the sender and receiver with artificial magnetic fields both before and during ESP tests," he said. "It gives them extra energy. The fields don't have to be strong. Weak fields work just as well."

The same geomagnetic parameters were used by Dr. Becker and his associates in 1964 to correlate the rise of admissions to psychiatric hospitals with magnetic storms, cosmic ray activity, and the Earth's electric current. The human organism *must* have regular levels of temperature and oxygen in order to survive and prosper, and there are also certain electromagnetic parameters beyond which organic life cannot adapt, survive, or function optimally.

In man's long search for a universal cure-all, none fits the description nearly as well as electromagnetic fields. The

American and Russian findings agree that the human central nervous system and brain depend on electrostatic charges for the organism's overall health and well-being. Serious consequences can result from insufficient negatively charged ions in the atmosphere.

A decade ago, hardly anyone dreamed that small amounts of electrical current applied to an amputated arm or leg would stimulate the cells to grow new tissue and limb muscle, nerve, and bone! Partial regeneration of amputated limbs seems awfully exotic, yet it's been done many times. Transplanting nerve tissue onto the amputated limb or even *injuring* the tissue at the site of the amputation seems to increase the flow of electrical current which promotes regrowth.

Exactly how *do* cells and tissues regroup themselves at the stump of an amputated limb? Is it part of the function of L-fields (the Fields of Life)? Becker thinks that the application of electrical current "may cause cells to revert to a primitive, undifferentiated (unspecialized) state, rather like the cells of an embryo. In some not-yet-understood manner, the undifferentiated cells become specialized once more and begin building new cells of their own type such as bone, muscle, skin and nerve."

But where do the mysterious "instructions" for resuming growth and specialization come from? "They might be provided by or through the central nervous system," Becker suggests, "or by the local cells. Even hormones might help in the specialization and regeneration process. Although we're working toward the total regeneration of amputated human limbs, it could be a long time coming."

Right now, he's more concerned with better understanding how cells and tissues repair themselves and in new ways to stimulate this process. "This way," he said, "we'll be on much firmer ground when we go all-out for total regeneration. We're trying to induce certain kinds of tissue to grow just a little *more* instead of scarring.

"For example, we might regrow the myocardium of damaged hearts. In some respects this is like 'cloning' whole organs. Let's say we suspect an individual might eventually suffer from a diseased or malfunctioning heart—or other organ. By taking a tissue culture and stimulating redifferentiation with a magnetic field or electric current, we could regrow a new, healthy organ and keep it in reserve for the time when a transplant might become necessary. Such a procedure would eliminate the problem of rejection because the original heart actually belongs to the patient himself.

"We could also remove severely damaged hip joints from patients, regenerate the damaged joint tissue and then reimplant the joint. I'm trying this procedure on dogs now."

Physically, the human brain is essentially an electromagnetic and chemical device, but as we'll see later, its functions are subject to the nonphysical mind. Small electric impulses applied to damaged brain areas will stimulate the nerves to activate muscles and also boost the healing process. Strong electric fields are generated when you splash water in a wash basin or take a shower. The positive charge runs down the drain, but the negative one stays in the atmosphere. This negatively ionized air probably accounts for more than 70 percent of the after-shower "lift" you experience. The same negative electrical differential makes trees and plants grow and thrive. Reverse its negative polarity and you can quickly kill a very large tree.

The reason city dwellers feel so refreshed and exhilarated after an outdoor holiday or vacation is largely because of the geomagnetic field. In large urban areas the Earth's electromagnetic field is effectively barred by large office buildings and apartments. The structures of modern civilization (including automobiles, trucks—even aircraft and ships) form Faraday cages, i.e., grounded metal boxes that neutralize the field. You feel tired and worn-out because your body *needs* a regular flow of electromagnetic energy.

Dr. Cristjo Cristofv, afther of the "Cristofv effect," invented an antifatigue device, a metal-enclosed can about the size of an orange, in which a solid-state device is connected to a battery. This is suspended from the ceiling on a slim probe and generates an 800-volt-per-meter field.

L. F. Tangemann, in the magazine *Product Engineering*, said, "Tests of pilots in high-flying reconnaisance planes and of truck drivers on the St. Louis–Milwaukee haul showed greater alertness and less tiredness when bathed in a negative magnetic field."

According to Cristofv himself, the 11-hour truck run was cut to eight hours and the drivers felt less tired and more able to sleep restfully afterward. Tests in factories and office buildings showed similar results.

"Metal isn't the only offender," according to Cristofv. Plastics also have an inherently high positive charge (*as high as 50,000 volts per meter!*), which degrades human performance and results in lowered resistance to illness and disease. He exposed cats to a positive field of this intensity; within three weeks their appetites dwindled to practically nothing, their sex drive evaporated, they became listless or sick, and even ran in terror from mice.

It was once believed that an increase in the dosage of cosmic radiation during times when the geomagnetic field was weakened was the cause of the inexplicable, wholesale, and sudden extinction of entire species and genera during the Earth's prehistoric past. New evidence however, points to the *direct* harmful effect of reduced magnetism on those creatures.

Whole continents were once plunged into conditions of zero magnetism. According to Dr. Robert J. Uffen of the University of Western Ontario, "There's clearly a causal relationship between geomagnetic reversals and the massive, sudden extinctions of whole species—many of them between 500 million and 250 million years ago."

No living thing on this planet—from microbes to whales—is immune to the beneficial or detrimental effects of magnetism. Evidence is increasing that *any* organism deprived of the Earth's magnetic field for a prolonged period will eventually suffer from numerous "mysterious" illnesses, ultimately resulting in crippling or death.

During comparatively recent periods of geological history there were numerous reversals of the magnetic *and* geographic poles. When this happens, the intensity of the geomagnetic field drops all the way to zero, then after a long interval, builds up to normal intensity. Studies revealed that it coincided with the massive extermination of everything from microbes to giant lizards at the end of the Ordovician period

(425 million years ago), the Devonian (345 million years), Triassic (180 million), and Cretaceous periods (65 million years ago).

In one study made by James D. Hays of Columbia University's Lamont-Doherty Geological Observatory, it was discovered that eight species of radiolaria (microscopic marine animals) became extinct immediately after each massive magnetic reversal.

During the reversal when magnetic intensity is near zero, cosmic radiation normally shielded out by the earth's magnetic field bathes the surface of the planet. Early on in the studies of the geomagnetic field, these radiations were believed to have produced mutations at a far greater speed and on a much wider scale than usual. "Many species perished," according to Dr. William B. F. Ryan of the Lamont-Doherty Laboratory, "simply because they were unable to adapt."

The trouble with this theory, according to Dr. C. J. Waddington of the University of Minnesota, is that the increase in cosmic radiation as a result of the removal of the magnetic field's shielding effect was entirely too small to have killed off any living creatures, even at sea level.

"The atmosphere between the equator and polar regions is so thick," he says, "that it would screen out any adverse cosmic radiation dosage." Ironically, the magnetic field is shaped in such a way that the polar regions are not shielded from radiation—*even when the field's intensity is at its maximum!* Since some of the exterminations happened in Antarctica, none of the magnetic reversals could have produced a noticeable increase in radiation dosage.

The most convincing evidence of the killing effect of low magnetism—*as opposed to increased cosmic radiation*—was presented by Ian K. Crain of Australia's National University. "This cosmic radiation theory" he said, "fails to explain how marine life, which is completely shielded from cosmic radiation by the density of the ocean's water, can be affected by increases of radiation in the atmosphere."

In spite of the all-but-conclusive proof of *Direct* extermination through loss of magnetism, there are hundreds of strange and exotic explanations for the mass extinction of ancient animals. One of these is that "magnetic reversals cause *climatic change* which has a negative influence on normal evolution."

Three Lamont-Doherty scientists matched changes in magnetic intensity with changes of climate for over a million-year period and concluded that *"a cause and effect relationship exists between changes in the Earth's magnetic field and the climate."*

According to Dr. William B. F. Ryan, "The higher the magnetic intensity, the colder the climate. Magnetism *could* change the climate by providing a shield against certain types of solar radiation." (Dr. Ryan used crustaceans, fish, and other marine life as his example.)

"Not so," retorted Australia's Ian Crane in a recent issue of the *Geological Society of America Bulletin.* "There's an enormous lag in thermal changes of the oceans. It could take centuries for a severe drop in atmospheric temperature to affect the ocean's temperature by even a few degrees! This gives marine life excellent protection from sudden changes in climate.

"There's a much simpler explanation for the correlation between magnetic reversals and mass extinctions of living things. *These are caused directly by the deadly effect of drastically reduced magnetism during each reversal!* Every study made on organisms living in magnetic fields of intensity *below* that of the Earth are extremely consistent. Every one of them shows enormous behavioral and physical abnormalities which are typical of life in a reduced magnetic field."

Is it conceivable that the long-range effect of decreased— or even zero—magnetism on our astronauts could be as deadly? According to Dr. Crain who has all the available evidence to back him, the answer is an emphatic "yes." Colonies of bacteria kept in a low magnetic field for only 72 hours suffered a drastic reduction in their reproductive capacity. Fifteen times less than normal, in fact.

In tests of reduced magnetism on mollusks, protozoans, and flatworms, scientists observed that their ability to move around or to reproduce was markedly decreased. Birds under the same conditions became disoriented; their motor activity was badly altered and their egg-laying capacity drastically lessened. Among mice and rats a decreased magnetic field adversely altered their enzyme activity. The longer each organism was deprived of magnetism, the less fertile it became, the more shriveled its tissues and organs and *the shorter its life span!*

"All things considered," says Dr. Crain, "the long-term effects of low magnetic fields must be considered absolutely lethal to *any* organism."

Strictly aside from their inner ear trouble and other physical complaints, the astronauts who have been to the Moon and back could form the nucleus for a whole new science. How many of these men, for example, will have fathered children since their return from the Moon? Dr. Charles A. Berry, a chief flight surgeon for NASA's astronauts bitterly complained that the top brass at the Manned Spacecraft Center in Houston flatly silenced him "when it came to talking about the rather serious medical problems encountered by the Apollo crews."

It would seem incredible if NASA scientists have not fully exploited and developed Dr. Cristofv's antifatigue magnetic field generator. According to official information however, none of the command modules in any of the Apollo flights ever used a supportive magnetic field.

As important as this is, even greater questions are posed by possibilities such as another geomagnetic reversal in the near future. Could the human race be wiped out like the dinosaurs by a wild fluctuation in the interplanetary and terrestrial field?

Such a geomagnetic reversal might mean the end of the history of Homo sapiens on this planet. If such a catastrophe did take place, it would be a subtle, almost unnoticed process. Without a warning, all arts, scientific knowledge, engineering achievements, and the entire span of human civilization would come to an end.

The first symptoms of the catastrophe would be a gradual decrease in travel and a growing disinterest by the general population in normal activities. Next, the almost incalculable effects of changes in the human enzymal system would affect the appetites and sexual activities of increasing millions of people. Wars would grind to a halt, diplomacy would shrivel and disappear, the food supply would dwindle as a result of changes in trade and commerce brought on by human ennui. The animal population of the land and seas would be decimated by a radical drop in reproductive and other abilities. There simply wouldn't be enough food to go around because plants would die off without the magnetic field.

Entire forests would wither away by prolonged deprivation of the magnetic field. This would affect the oxygen supply in the atmosphere, thus intensifying all other negative effects on the human race. By comparison, present-day ecological problems would be insignificant.

"Magnetic fields," Dr. Crain pointed out, "would operate with equal effectiveness on marine and terrestrial organisms because water doesn't act as a barrier against them. A radical drop in geomagnetic intensity would be far more deadly than any increase in cosmic ray dosage. It would have a more *lasting* lethal effect on the most complex organisms, for instance, than on lower forms such as reptiles, insects or bacteria."

Scientists still don't know the exact mechanisms involved in the extermination of species. "Biomagnetic changes *could* come from electrical reactions between the geomagnetic field and the ions in living cells," Dr. Crain suggests. "The total effect could easily be as catastrophic as the existing fossil record indicates it was."

The end of the human race is about the most dismal prospect imaginable. But what of the idea of a *new* species of intelligent creature existing millions of years from now? A species puzzling over the discovery of thousands of *human* instead of dinosaur fossils? Could it happen?

Possibly. It has before. But considering the time required for geomagnetism to drop to zero, we might be able to prepare for it. With a vastly expanded knowledge of solar magnetism, the interplanetary magnetic field, and terrestrial magnetic effects on life, chances are that we'd be quickly alerted to any magnetic anomaly. This is one edge the dinosaurs didn't have.

It's possible—even probable—that human ingenuity would eventually develop artificial fields. They'd be larger and more powerful than anything yet conceived—individual shields to blanket homes and factories. Entire cities, farms, and forests could be bathed in artificially generated fields. Huge activators might even be constructed on the oceans' floors to protect marine life!

Even without this sword of Damocles hanging over our collective heads, the rewards to be gained from full-scale research in this most-important science could be incalculable. It could become the most important thrust of collective human effort ever made.

Chapter Seven

The Brain

Thomas Wolfe (the lesser), spokesman for the "new journalism," has gone "ape" about the workings of the human brain:

"Brain physiology really fascinates me," he said in a recent magazine interview. *"The brain seems to be a great yes-no mechanism ... There's some great stuff coming out of the current interest in brain physiology. The idea that people's minds can be controlled through this kind of research—such as these transistorized units that can be imbedded in your skull to control certain things, or a pill that can control our actions—this doesn't interest me at all. This is scare stuff. What does interest me is the horrible possibility that people might actually understand their own minds, the workings of their own minds ... That's going to be a really, really horrifying boundary to cross. It really will be. It'll so shake people when these things are understood. Can you imagine? When the whole chess game is figured out?"**

At best, this is extremely unlikely. All available data indicates that the human brain is so "programmed" as to be forever incapable of omniscience—of comprehending everything.

We're not quite ready for godhood; to think we are seems to be the rankest kind of human chauvinism. The Universe, with its infinite number of intriguing mysteries is infinitely more than a game of chess. Unless we've actually created ourselves, it's extremely doubtful that the secrets of the Universe can ever be fathomed by the three pounds of pinkish-gray jelly we call the brain.

**Writer's Digest*, September, 1974.

Not a single one of the 2500 delegates at the Twenty-first International Congress of Psychology could explain the workings of the Mind in terms of the brain. Sir Charles Sherrington, the great English physiologist, who studied brains for many years, finally concluded that "No chemical or electronic drill or scalpel has yet discovered what center of the cerebral cortex in the civilized brain produces compassion, tact or good taste."

Compared to the best knowledge we now have of the human body and its functions, almost *nothing* has been learned about the brain since the time of Hippocrates. The brain is believed to be the seat of personality, intelligence, character, and a host of other intangibles, but scientists can't explain how the brain manifests these attributes. The brains and nervous systems of most animals are extremely susceptible to genetic manipulation and cloning. Cells taken from the brains of animals (or humans) will, if the conditions are right, reassemble themselves in a nutrient culture to form "mini-brains" which are just as functional as the originals, according to Dr. Nicholas Seeds, assistant professor of the Department of Biophysics and Genetics at the University of Colorado Medical Center. On the face of it, this seems to have the chilling overtones of Orwell's 1984, yet the basic facts have been known since 1894.

Scientists at the University of California at Irvine recently demonstrated that the brain is capable of "rewiring" itself, even after severe injury. Professors Gary Lynch and Carl Cotman of the UCI School of Biological Sciences reported, "The brain has an amazing and heretofore unsuspected capability for *reorganization* after brain damage." Although this is extremely interesting, it isn't *too* surprising because it's been suspected for at least 80 years.

The question is, *how* does the brain "rewire" itself? Are the cells and molecules of which it is composed "smarter" than the brain as a whole? Can the brain "know itself" and deliberately make these repairs? Do "you" determine the activity of your brain—or vice-versa? Where is the essence of the personality?

Nowhere in the brain or body is there an answer to any of

these questions. Intelligence and Consciousness therefore, must lie somewhere else.

According to Professor (of behavioral biology) James Polidora at the University of California, Davis, School of Medicine, "this three pounds of pinkish-grey jelly is the most mysterious known organ in the Universe."

There's now a kind of renaissance of the neurosciences (brain physiology), which is being described as "man's most valuable frontier."

At a recent meeting of the American Association for the Advancement of Science, Dr. Robert B. Livingston told his audience, "When man better understands the biological, psychological and cultural mechanisms affecting his perceptions and learning—the mechanisms of image formation—he will have more substantial grounds than religious, political and moral imperatives for empathy, tolerance and tentativeness of judgement.

"He will gain more reliable means for predicting and shaping the social consequences of his actions, and will be better equipped to cope with confrontations, both individual and international."

That's a tall order, but certainly well within our grasp. Dr. Livingston's basic theme lies in the natural ability of the human brain to arrange (and classify) sensory experiences, motor performances, and social communications and to provide for a capacity for expanded learning.

Oddly enough, in certain specific areas of brain activity, many animals far outstrip human capabilities. According to Livingston, "the main difference between man and animal is that man is not locked into a system of immediate reaction to a specific situation. He is free to look at the situation, judge it, examine alternatives and only *then*, to act." Image formation, apparently, is of prime importance to human survival. It accumulates according to past experience and is of controlling significance in processes of perception, judgement, language, behavior, "and in other far-reaching conditions affecting mankind."

How then, did the Earth's animal population—without image formation—manage to survive? The more primitive the brain, scientists claim, the less capable the organism is to survive. The University of California at San Diego has a new Center for Human Information Processing. An intensive study is underway to learn 1) how the brain works, 2) how we develop intellectual skills, 3) how the brain receives and stores information, 4) how sensory information is registered, 5) how the brain recalls data when needed, and 6) how it assembles bits of information in reaching a conclusion or making a decision.

According to John Mihalasky, an associate professor of management engineering at the Newark College of Engineering, most big corporate decisions are totally illogical! Paradoxically, he observed, the vast majority of these hunches or intuitive decisions made by executives turned out to be *right!* Professor Mihalasky has a strong scientific bent plus degrees in both management and engineering, so he figured there *had* to be a logical answer to this apparent contradiction.

After long and fruitful study he came to the conclusion that top echelon decisions are much broader (therefore based on less precise information and with little benefit of solid facts) than decisions at lower management levels. On the premise that logical people can understand a "scientific" explanation of an illogical process, he devised and carried out a series of experiments that eventually demonstrated that there was a strong and definite correlation between superior management ability and an executive's extrasensory perception! (The Newark College of Engineering has been doing ESP research since 1962.)

Whatever force or energy governs extrasensory perception, however, can't be found *anywhere* in the brain, so it must originate from another source. "What are the chemical or neurological or anatomical substrates of the evocative ghosts we call 'memories'?" Professor David Krech wanted to know. "After millenia of philosophical debate, centuries of hard thinking and decades of scientific research, we know almost next to nothing about that question," he said. For his outstanding work on the brain, Professor Krech was honored with an award by the International Forum for Neurological Organization.

Professor Krech managed to discover that the more it is used, the bigger, heavier, and healthier the brain grows. "The brain stimulated for long periods in an enriched environment—and presumably, therefore, with many more stored memories," he said, "has a heavier and thicker cortex, a better blood supply, larger brain cells, more glia cells and increased activity of two brain enzymes than does the brain from a human or animal whose life has been less memorable."

There's just no comparison however, between the intellectual capacity of an animal and that of a human being. Brain size has long been considered a criterion of intelligence, and human thought *is* vastly superior to animal thought. Evolutionists believe it's due to the fact that the human brain itself is more advanced. But is it? Can the difference between human and animal brains account for the incredible gulf that exists between an animal and human mental activity? Is human intellect completely controlled by the brain?

The evidence says not.

Using brain size and weight on a proportionately decreasing scale, the brains of a whale, elephant, and dolphin are much larger and heavier than that of a man. All large mammalian brains look pretty much alike; they all have the same distinctive brain structure: the cerebellum, spinal cord, midbrain, medulla, hypothalami, thalami, corpus callosum, cerebral cortex, and so on. *Physically,* the brain of a human being is unprepossessing; it's just not all that unique.

In one sense, thoughts are like microelectric charges, passed along as nerve impulses by neurons, the basic component of all nervous systems.

The neurons of all other mammals, including chimpanzees, dogs, cats, rats, mice, are identical to the neurons of human beings. Dendrites, those branching matrices of neuron antennae, are more numerous and complex among creatures higher on the evolutionary scale. The more dendrite branches there are, the greater number of connections and pathways there are to associate the billions of neurons, hence a greater complexity of mental options is available to that particular brain.

The branching dendrites are most complex in man, but very closely followed by the dolphin and chimpanzee. By comparing the numberless "dendritic spines," making comparative biochemical analyses, and studying the chemical mechanisms of all mammalian nerve fibers, scientists concluded that, "Biochemically, at any rate, the brains of all large mammals are essentially the same."

Compared to some animals, man doesn't have a particularly large brain. In fact, every physical characteristic of the human brain is found *easily* in the brains of all other mammals. Aha! But the brain operates by its constant electrochemical action, so the critical question has to be, "is the human brain's *electrochemical* activity noticeably superior to that of the animals?"

Surprisingly not. In electroencephalograms (EEG), i.e., tracings of the electrical patterns made by the brain, human (and animal) patterns during relaxed and alert periods are virtually indistinguishable! By using very wide comparisons and measurements, it can be shown that the brain of a human being is only slightly more complex than that of a porpoise, a chimpanzee, or whale.

But there's another surprise—if intellectual capacity were based on studies of the physical brain alone, man would be only a notch or two above chimps, dolphins, and whales. Yet by comparison of relative achievements, human beings are so *totally* different from all other creatures that man is obviously in a class all by himself. As far as we now know (the evidence on dolphins and whales is not complete, by any means), man and *only* man is capable of communicating symbolically, i.e., with language, art, music. Of all the creatures that emerged from "the dim mists of Darwinian evolution," man is the only one to question his own existence, to wonder how he came into being, to inquire about his origin, his future, his very *purpose*. No animal that ever existed has ever been known to have time orientation, to appreciate beauty, to become angry, to laugh, to build great civilizations, to wage war, or to pass on the accumulated knowledge of one generation to the next.

Animals don't engage in warfare. What is there about the human brain that makes so vast a difference in the quality of excellence of performance when compared with the performance of animals? Some new or undiscovered anatomical structure or unique functional principle would seem to be involved. Yet thousands of human and animal brains have been studied, dissected, and thoroughly analyzed, and this factor has never been found.

The disturbing fact is that the brains of man and animal are *not all that different!* To an untrained observer it would be impossible to tell the difference between the brain of a porpoise and that of a man. The brain of a gorilla is about as superior to that of a dog as man's would be to the ape's. On a scale of increasing complexity, the rat's brain is *inferior* to that of a dog, but an ape's brain is more complex and therefore superior to *both*. In each and every case, however, the progressive complexity of the physical brains of animals is reflected by higher forms of mental (and physical) activity. A study of the brains of animals completely accounts for their total behavior and *all* their mental activity.

If the brains of a rat, dog, gorilla, and man were shown to a hypothetical intelligent being from another planet and this alien studied only the habits and activity of *the animals*, he would be forced to conclude (from the evidence of the brains alone) that man was also an animal—only *slightly* superior to the ape, and therefore would be expected to be only *slightly* better than the simian at mental activity.

This stupendous gap in the quality and quantity of mental activity between man and the next highest primate is simply astounding. There's just no accounting for it. The theory of behaviorists therefore, who claim that *all human mental activity* is solely and exclusively generated by the human brain is mostly *dead wrong*.

There is something totally unique about being human—something that can't be measured, dissected, weighed, or even directly detected. Some unique, undiscovered, *nonphysical* component must somehow coexist in and with the human body and brain. YOU are the biggest mystery you'll ever encounter because your own brain is *incapable* of explaining your mind or the forces that motivate you.

The Plain Truth, a publication of the Ambassador College in Pasadena, California (which is free for the asking, by the way), flatly states that "a nonphysical addition must unite with and augment the human brain, converting it into the human mind, making it capable of abstract, cognitive, deductive, inductive and symbolic thought."

Without this nonphysical component of the human mind, man would be nothing more than a "super chimp," more intelligent than a normal chimpanzee to the same *limited* degree that a "normal" chimp is more intelligent than a cat or dog—not much.

What is Mind? How is it generated? There are no answers to these questions; we can only infer that man is governed by a nonphysical Mind which makes him totally different from all other creatures.

Whales, dolphins, and elephants have huge, well-structured brains—much larger than the brain of man. The brain of the elephant is smaller than that of the whale, which can tip the scales at nearly 20 pounds—six times heavier than the three-pound brain of the average human being.

Brain size and weight alone reveal little and prove nothing about intelligence. If it did, an elephant would be three times more intelligent than a man and the intellect of a whale would be as far beyond our comprehension as ours is to a mouse. Originally, these vast differences puzzled naturalists who insisted that the human brain fully explained man's position as the lord of creation.

But then another group of researchers came up with a theory that seemed to save the materialistic belief. It wasn't the weight of the brain itself that mattered, they claimed, but the brain's weight *in proportion* to total body weight. On such a scale, man's brain-to-body ratio is 1.8 per cent, which convinced them that—despite the much bigger brains of whales, porpoises, and elephants—the theory comfortably explained human intellectual dominance.

But look what this did to the poor cetaceans! Whales and porpoises are known to be almost indistinguishable in intelligence and ability, yet the average porpoise brain is 0.86 per cent of its body weight as compared to 0.005 per cent for a blue whale! This would make the porpoise and dolphin more than 200 times as intelligent as the whale! Moreover—according to the brain/body-weight ratio, man would be only *twice* as smart as a porpoise.

The idea is all wet; on this scale the dolphin, porpoise,

whale, *and* man would all take an intellectual back seat to the little South American capuchin monkey whose brain is a whopping 5.7 per cent of its total body weight—*more than 200 percent above the human brain/body-weight ratio!* The researchers were hard put to see anything the monkey did to justify their theory.

Undaunted, they then reasoned that since *the entire brain* wasn't responsible for consciousness, personality, and intelligence, it must be the *cerebral cortex*, the convoluted outermost layer of the brain, about one sixth of an inch thick, that contains billions of nerve cells. Its furrowed, folded convolutions serve the purpose of compacting a large surface area into a small volume. The same principle is found throughout the human body and among all living things, including land and marine animals, trees and plants. Our lungs, for example, display the same branching principle as trees; this permits maximum dispersion (of lungs) to blood and oxygen and of trees to sunlight and carbon dioxide.

Professor E. J. Slijper compared the specific sensory projection cortex (which receives, analyzes, and processes direct sensory information—i.e., seeing, hearing, and feeling) and tried to show that this was what made man superior to all other animals.*

When that didn't work either, he compared the *intrinsic cortex* of man's brain which has no direct contact with the outside environment to a similar area of the whale's brain. That didn't prove anything, so he figured that it must be the ratio of *intrinsic* cortex (presumably the area governing human thought and therefore the highest mental activities) to the *total* cortex which explained man's vast superiority.

But it turned out that whales and dolphins have an even *greater* amount of intrinsic cortex than human beings! "[The] cetacean brain," Professor Slijper then hypothesized, "extends so far back that in the common dolphin it completely covers the cerebellum at the rear of the cranial cavity. Their cerebral cortexes are exceptionally convoluted. These convolutions are not only very striking in appearance,

*E. J. Slijper, *Whales,* Basic Books, New York, 1962.

but are an essential criterion for judging the stage of development a given brain has reached."

He nearly proved that the highly developed brains of sperm whales and dolphins gave them *the same brain capacity* as that of man.

But not the same capacity of Mind, which is *non*physical, like the L-field, but on a higher, more "refined" level.

In "Whales, Dolphins and Porpoises," Lawrence Kruger also proved that the intrinsic cortex of dolphins was almost the same as that of man. Another theory that attempted to explain human superiority (strictly in terms of the physical brain) was that the molecular layer (the top layer) of the cerebral cortex was much thicker in man than any other animal.

Kruger debunked this theory; the molecular layer of dolphins and whales ranges from 350 to 500 microns, which is in the same category as that of man and more than double the thickness of this layer in all comparable animals.

The controversy raged back and forth. The neurophysiologists could never understand why the huge, extremely complex cetacean brains didn't give the aquatic mammals total psychological dominance over all other terrestrial life forms.

Creativity may be the key to an answer. Animals don't write music, create paintings, or build civilizations. They don't choose up sides to kill their own kind, either.

Where *do* ideas come from? Some of the great scientific discoveries in history originated in a flash of "illumination." The famous German organic chemist, Friedrich August Kekulé, for example, *dreamed* of the precise ring structure for the carbon compound, benzene! Modern organic chemistry is solidly based on this fundamental concept. Was Kekulé's dream the work of his *brain* or some less tangible manifestation of creative energy?

How is the physical brain involved in feats of extrasensory perception? There's absolutely nothing physical about the "mess of gray porridge" we carry around inside our skulls to explain what it is that makes us so special. If tact, compassion, and other higher emotional/intellectual attributes are not the direct result of the brain's electrochemical activity, then these higher attributes *must* originate in some nonphysical dimension. Of all the creatures on Earth, only man seems aware of being "connected" to a higher form of energy or field. This may be the etheric medium which enables man to influence plants with his mind and connects us to each other and all living things.

Several natural philosophers of classic Greek antiquity postulated an eternal hierarchy of ever-greater fields or dimensions composed of countless numbers of miniscule energy "charges." This may now help us to understand how the L-fields of human beings are so intimately involved with the physical matter of our bodies and brains.

The miracle of this mysterious "bond" between matter and energy may be fundamentally unsolvable. Our brains may be programmed to *suspect* the powerful, subtle matter/energy interaction of this field *without* being able to comprehend it at all. We don't know *how* the brain thinks, let alone *why*. We haven't learned whether mind is the seat of the personality or the "soul" of the individual. The brain is marvelous and wonderful beyond imagination. Despite its countless myriads of nerves and dendrites, its synapses, and incredibly complex system of governing switches that constantly supervise the *physical* activity of the organism, the brain is a poor candidate as a storage bin for the overriding Mind or soul.

Maybe the brain acts as a kind of receiver-transformer, temporarily translating the most basic leitmotif—from let's call it (for lack of a better or more accurate term) the higher Self—into subliminal feelings and subconscious urgings that influence (in the most general way) the direction and quality of our lives. Be that as it may, the brain is the only known *physical* manifestation of the intellect.

In the remote past men believed that emotion was felt with their hearts and that intelligence was found in the stomach. For all practical purposes, the brain in design and function is a vastly more superior physical mechanism than the most sophisticated and fastest computers ever constructed. This might not always be so. Machines have *already* been developed with extremely high intelligence and consciousness. The Artificial Intelligence Group at M.I.T., for example, has successfully built and programmed computer systems that interact and "talk" to each other at light speed. Many are capable of learning from their own mistakes and correcting them. Others, built to relieve human workers of tedious and monotonous jobs, are equipped with decision-making apparatus. There are even freewheeling (or walking) robots programmed with fundamental sensors that enable them to make instantaneous decisions from myriads of multiple-choice selections. For all intents and purposes, these robots have much more free will than cats or dogs. And the robots are infinitely smarter.

In this sense, the brain is on about the same level as an electronic computer. The late Dr. Norbert Weiner, M.I.T.'s pioneering cybernetician, predicted the development and evolution of machines as *superior* to us as we are to the lower animals. Such devices are definitely on the way. The question raised with increasing frequency is, "Will we be able to control them?"

In experiments on animals, the brains of rats, cats, dogs, and monkeys were surgically separated along their vertical axes, i.e., the two hemispheres were sliced apart. These areas are believed to govern all the body's motor and intellectual/emotional functions. Among humans, "split-brained" people's hemispheres were also surgically cleft into two distinct halves. The left half controls the right side of the body and vice versa. The right half (which controls the left side) is more emotional and primitive than the other.

The results of these separations are often quite bizarre. For some unknown reason, the right half of one man's severed brain suddenly developed an intense dislike for his wife. According to a straight-faced report in *Scientific American*, "His left hand was continually making obscene gestures at her and once tried to strangle her. Only by using his stronger right hand could he break the grip of his left to keep from killing her."

Modern psychosurgery and other intrusions into the brain are wreaking havoc on our long-cherished belief in free will.

Dr. John Eccles (professor of physiology and biophysics at the Medical School of the State University of New York at Buffalo) is a staunch believer in free will. "I have indubitable experience that by wishing and thinking I can affect my actions," he said. This might be called the ontological proof of free will. "It exists because we can imagine and experience its existence."

But does it? The purely materialistic scientists—in fact all of sciencedom—operates on the objective evidence that we exist in a Universe of inviolable law, so how can free will be part of a deterministic Universe?

"Granted," said Professor Eccles, "it's a terrible nightmare. But we have strong evidence that Mind—insofar as consciousness and dispositional intentions are concerned—can affect the world of physical objects and physiological processes. I can give no scientific account of how thinking affects action," he said at an interdisciplinary conference of physicists and physiologists at the University of Miami in 1974. "We're getting on with the job but still have far to go."

Eccles estimates that 98 percent of our actions are not free-willed, but automatic. There are advantages in this. No creature, including man, could function if we had to consciously will our hearts to keep beating while we breathed, walked, digested our food, and carried on the millions of tasks that the brain and/or mind now does automatically. Yet some yogis have demonstrated that will *can* invade and take over many previously unconscious automatic activities of the body, including control of blood flow, slowing the heartbeat and respiration to an almost dead standstill, and the like.

To demonstrate the control of mind over physical matter just "will" your arm to rise. The *thought* is immediately followed by the action, but how? The mystery tantalizing Professor Eccles and his colleagues now is: how does nonphysical *thought* fire the parametal cells of the motor cortex in the brain? Scientists know that this action triggers a long chain of firing down the neural pathways of the brain to the appropriate muscles. "But what goes on before the parametal cells fire?" Eccles wants to know.

"We've got to look for the place where the brain is in direct contact with the conscious self," he says. "It helps to study people whose brains have been surgically split."

In modern psychosurgery, brain-splitting, or severing the two hemispheres, is a desperate, last-ditch resort for patients who suffer three to five severe epileptic seizures a day. "When all drugs fail," says John Eccles, "these people come to us begging for help."

After a patient's brain has been surgically split, the left hand quite literally doesn't know what the right hand is doing, or—more accurately—it's the right hand that really "knows"; the left hand is a great copier, a sort of automatic writer. Split-brained people are out of volitional control and contact with their left sides. The man whose left hand tried to strangle his wife is typical of the fact that in many cases the right side of the brain displays negative and nasty traits of character. Some experts theorize that the right brain's "evil" tendencies are somehow caused by terrible frustration because of its speechlessness—*the right brain is believed to be mute*. Even among left-handed persons who are right-brained in other things, the speech areas seem to be located in the left brain. And man is the *only* animal whose brain possesses speech areas.

Rationality, therefore, is intimately involved with speech. We reason, talk, and communicate with *words*. And except for lightning-like flashes of "illumination" or intuition, we even tend to *think* in words. It seems logical then that it is the left brain which is in constant contact with the consciousness, the higher Self, the soul, L-field, or Atman.

"But at what stage of the physiological action does rationality and free will crowbar themselves into this world of snapping and firing neurons?" Professor Eccles wondered.

According to the renowned British physicist Sir Arthur Eddington, free will and consequently nonphysical Mind might be accounted for by the "Uncertainty Principle," which forms the basis of quantum mechanics.

This means that in quantum mechanics, which rules the world of atomic and subatomic particle physics, no specific initial conditions necessarily lead directly to one and only one end—as in other areas of physics. As an example, let's say you're answering a series of multiple-choice questions for a test. Each correct answer is the *key* to the next multiple-choice question and so on. You have no way of knowing whether you've actually picked the correct answer because either way you're allowed to proceed to the next question.

According to our somewhat limited way of thinking such a

test seems eminently unfair. If you answered 99 out of a hundred questions right and the wrong answer was the *first* one, you'd already have taken the wrong fork in the road, and the next 99 correct answers wouldn't count. Even if the situation were reversed, and the *wrong* answer was the *last one*, the result would be the same—you'd flunk the test.

This is a fair analogy of conditions in the Real Universe however. Like a bullet that begins to fall as soon as it's fired from a gun, the beginning of life must inevitably end in the death of the *physical* organism. Science is finally beginning to remove the shackles of materialism that for several centuries have stifled man's natural curiosity about existence, consciousness, intelligence, and human creativity. The hesitant stamp of approval for the study of psionics, radiesthesia, and all forms of human ESP by government, academic, and scientific authorities is just the tip of the iceberg of a profound evolutionary change in human consciousness and civilization. Socially, politically, and psychically, we're becoming an entirely different species—and for very good reasons.

Studies of the L-field and other refined forms of energy strongly suggest that these nonphysical forces which animate the brains and bodies of the entire human species do *not* perish when our bodies and brains cease to function at death. Physical oblivion and dissolution is *not* the goal of life, but a portal of exit for consciousness and personality into another plane echelon of existence, or dimension. Few people have had the opportunity of surviving to tell about this transcendental experience. In every case, however, it is described as knowledge of an ecstatically beautiful and blissful condition for which our language has no words and our physical brains no concepts.

Be it remembered, however, that every society that has survived more than two generations has, in one form or another, had three things in common: 1) laws and rules regulating the behavior of the sexes, 2) a viable system of agriculture and barter, and 3) a strong belief in a Supreme Being (or Beings) and the immortality of the human soul—even the most primitive social groups.

As William Inge ("the gloomy dean") said in *The Fall of*

*the Idols,** "Every institution not only carries with it the seeds of its own dissolution, but also prepares the way for its most hated rival."

That's a good description of the character and effect of the Victorian era, of nineteenth-century scientific materialism and colonialism. Today, in the so-called "Aquarian Age" of alleged freedom from social, political, sexual, financial, and racial oppression and at the dawn of interstellar communication with other civilizations and colonization of other planets—the most advanced elements of science and technology are finally beginning to accept ideas and philosophies that the majority of our human ancestors either strongly suspected or fervently believed.

One of these dogmas is that man is much more than a mere physical organism. We all exist and are part of what appears to be a deterministic Universe, a condition that severely limits our choices. If we're actually part of a vast "machine" constructed to function in predetermined ways for a specific end, then we can foresee only a miniscule part of the immediate future. No human engineer in his right mind would design a complex engine and allow several nuts and bolts to rattle around freely inside. Any elements within such an engine which didn't conform to its overall purpose could easily destroy it.

From the foregoing, let's draw an analogy: it is conceivable that if each and every human being were able to express total freedom of choice, it would only be a matter of time before another disciplined maniac like Hitler would gain control of a nation with the nuclear means of destroying all life on the planet. But this *hasn't* happened, and all indications are that it *won't* happen. In a future war humanity conceivably could bomb itself back into the Stone Age (again?)—*if* life was created to be destroyed.

In the deterministic Universe our senses are unable to detect all wavelengths of energy, and the brain cannot comprehend the meaning of everything it perceives. It isn't the brain that prompts us to probe the unknown. An intimate intercausal relationship triggers the urge to explore the planets

*William Inge, *The Fall of the Idols,* Cambridge University Press, New York, c. 1940.

and stars while at the same time we're engaged in an exciting all-out, planet-wide revolution of psychic discovery. One is prerequisite to the other. They're manifestations of the invisible forces that have guided the human race to the threshhold of space. Even now it is clear that *species maturity* is the next inevitable step before homo sapiens is "qualified" for interspecies contact.

The entire human race is being shoved along a predetermined path by billions of converging lines of force leading to our becoming a spacefaring race. Apparently we have little or no choice in the matter. The number of options available to an organ, an organism, or an entire species *decreases* in direct ratio to its increased complexity and specialization.

We're unconsciously conforming to the urge felt by the Mass Human Consciousness to leave the cradle of our adolescence. We're hardly even conscious of the urge. Despite our most cherished convictions, the physical brain cannot initiate anything; rather, it *responds* to stimulation by higher energies in much the same way as radio-controlled robots and vehicles like Russia's Lunokhod and America's Viking Mars landers. Human hands built and powered these devices. Human minds instructed them to explore hostile worlds where human flesh would find it difficult to survive.

We've answered almost 95 percent of the hypothetical "multiple-choice questions" correctly, but we still face the old Uncertainty Principle of the physicists. If it were possible to deviate from our predetermined path, our next wrong answer—our refusal, say, to accept the challenge of space exploration—could cause a cultural and economic relapse that would plunge civilization back into medieval or even a Stone Age level of existence.

In such a case, mankind might suffer from a form of collective amnesia. Our descendants in the remote future would then be forced to begin all over under conditions similar to those preceding the Industrial Revolution. They'd have no memory of past accomplishments or past greatness, no knowledge of scientific advances or technological wizardry.

Such a possibility can't be lightly dismissed. It could be a description of events that happened on Earth during pre-biblical days. Ten thousand years ago human beings had seen the rise and fall of hundreds of great civilizations. Men, women, and children like ourselves had already existed for many hundreds of thousands of years. There may have been civilizations as advanced as our own a million years before Christ.

That's not as bizarre as it seems. The latest fossil records of early man were recently pushed back an *additional* 2 million years. This updated the 1962 discovery of anthropologist Louis S. B. Leakey when he electrified the world with his discovery (in the Olduvai Gorge in Tanzania, and Lake Rudolph in Kenya, Africa) of the remains of human beings dated at from 2 to 2½ million years old.

Then in October 1974, a four-nation research expedition to North-Central Ethiopia sponsored by Cleveland's Case Western Reserve University and the French National Center for Scientific Research, discovered fossilized human bones *"at least four million years old."*

A debate now rages over whether the bones belonged to "true man" or "near man"—a moot point, apparently. Four million years ago genus Homo walked upright, he was "a tool-making, meat-eating entity," according to Drs. Carl Johnson and Maurice Taieb, "who had some kind of cooperative social structure and a good system of communication."

In other words, *a spoken language. Homo sapiens* is the only animal whose brain possesses speech areas. The conclusion is obvious.

"All previous theories of the origin of the lineage which leads to modern man must now be totally revised," they announced. "We must now throw out many existing theories and consider the possibility that Man's origins go back to well over four million years." Later data has pushed this figure to an estimated 10 million years.

That's a long time for evolution to work its changes, if any, on the human race. Where are the civilizations, say, of just *half* a million years ago? How many times has mankind reached (or surpassed) the present stage of scientific advancement? What about Atlantis? Lemuria? Mu? Hyperborea?

The fantasy and legend of yesteryear is becoming the fact of today. Such ideas are slowly percolating up through the Mass Human Consciousness to galvanize our brains and influence our behavior. It's as though we're being programmed to soften the intellectual and emotional shock of contact with several species of intelligent, nonhuman beings—creatures either too alien for our brains to comprehend or as familiar as long-lost brothers.

Astronomers estimate that there are probably as many civilizations in our Milky Way Galaxy as there are seeds that fall from the trees of a hundred thousand orchards. The revolution propelling the human species to evolve into Genus Terran is forcing the development of our latent nonphysical talents and abilities in order to transcend the limitations of our material brains.

Waiting for us far off in space are beauties beyond belief, wonders beyond imagination and life forms totally beyond our present comprehension. There are exquisite worlds, strange solar systems, galaxies of stars and planets, and clusters of galaxies of suns and worlds and endless, showering ebullitions of all these and more—pouring and whirling forever outward into space and through time and timelessness—numberless worlds many times more beautiful in spirit than our own lovely blue sphere—where enlightened beings express unfathomable dreams and unimaginable joys grow and flower and fulfill themselves in three-dimensional paradises under living heavens beyond the limits of our brains and yet—quite literally—right before our eyes and within our minds and hearts.

Chapter Eight

Genus Terran

"I speak of my brain as if it were a computer. It is."

R. BUCKMINSTER FULLER

An average high-speed computer can make more than 4 million additions of 36-figure numbers per second. In many ways these machines are vastly superior to the human brain. In hours it can solve problems so complex that a team of highly trained human mathematicians would require scores—perhaps hundreds—of centuries to complete.

The impact these machines have had and will continue to have on civilization is incalculable. Future historians will have recorded that toward the end of the twentieth century man created and introduced a true catalyst into his complex culture. (Those historians may not necessarily be human.) On a technological level civilization is advancing as much in one year now as it did in a hundred years during the eighteenth century.

A computer with all its associated equipment can occupy as many as three entire floors of a large building in a space complex such as NASA's Mission Control Center in Houston. The average large-size computer contains millions of parts, including countless miles of wiring. Ostensibly, we understand how computers work and are familiar with their parts because they are our own invention. Some evolutionists see the "thinking machine" as the most perfect vessel to house intelligence. In their view, man is simply the tool needed to begin the evolution of machines, and consequently merits no other explanation. In contrast to the impressive statistics about artificial intelligence, man's brain is more complex and versatile

124

than any computer it has ever created. With its astonishingly complex interconnections—more than 10 thousand million nerve cells—the human brain remains an enigma.

We can easily understand how a computer's magnetic tapes record and "memorize" scores of billions of bits of information, yet no one can explain how the human brain can remember that 5 plus 5 equals 10.

In 1825 a French anatomist named Franz Joseph Gall published an enormous six-volume work in which he assigned nearly every aspect of human existence to some part of the physical brain, even to such abstract concepts as "the instinct for the continuation of the race, bravery, love of children, manual dexterity, thriftiness," and so on.

Although modern anatomists, neurologists, and brain physiologists claim to know which parts of the brain are involved in walking, breathing, or raising a hand, they can't figure out what happens inside the brain when we remember, dream, imagine, or reason. Such research seems to cross the borderline of mysticism.

The sensory mechanisms—skin, eyes, ears, tongue, and nose—provide the brain with great masses of data about the outside environment. It seems—or is made to seem—to us only natural that the brain is "packaged" inside the head, so close to the sensory organs. It demonstrates Nature's foresight and marvelous economy, but there are other mysteries.

For example, can the brain actually "know" itself? The search for identity and intelligence *solely in the brain* has proved to be either elusive or futile. Even when we are sleeping, more than 50 *million* nerve messages are being relayed back and forth between the brain and different parts of the body each second. Scientists are not at all certain that the brain *alone* is responsible for keeping our hearts beating, our lungs supplied with oxygen, our bodies at constant temperature, etc. Orthodox anatomy and physiology—steeped in the dogma of Darwinism—have never been able to determine the "mechanism" by which this balance is maintained and controlled. So far, no one in any of these fields has accepted the evidence pointing to the existence of the overriding, nonphysical L-field.

As we've seen, brain size alone has little or nothing to do

with intelligence. A woman's brain is generally smaller than a man's, but who would dare suggest that Gloria Steinem, Bella Abzug, or Betty Friedan are less intelligent than William F. Buckley, Tom Wolfe, or Rex Reed? Anatole France, the brilliant French philosopher, was practically a pin head, and the heaviest human brain ever weighed belonged to a congenital idiot.

Nerve cells (called neurons) are the basic physical units which make up the brain and nervous system. These are round, oval, or spindle-shaped cells that measure about a thousandth of an inch across and always carry a tiny electrical charge—*even when not stimulated*. (So far, no one has ventured a guess as to what happens at death. Is the "juice" switched off suddenly or does it fade gradually?)

The electrical charge is generated by the chemical difference/interaction between the inside of the nerve cell and the surrounding tissue. When you touch or taste something there's a change in the chemical balance which causes an electrical charge. In effect, the neuron "fires."

This is the *electrochemical* method of producing electricity; one neuron starts an entire series of its neighboring nerve cells to "fire" in rapid succession so that an electrical impulse flows along the nerve fiber the way a spark burns up a long corded fuse—except that it's much faster. Every second, even as you read these lines, millions of neurons are firing throughout your body and these electrical impulses, which travel at nearly the speed of light itself, quickly reach your brain. The brain is supposed to "sort out" these electric charges like the nerve center of a large solid-state computer, and "reject" the trivial or unimportant ones according to the classic model (which doesn't explain *how* it goes about this task).

The brain-body relationship then, is a symbiotic/cybernetic one. It receives *priority* messages and returns additional impulses to the body in the form of commands. As you reach for a pencil or pen, your eye flashes the picture of your hand and the distance to the object to your brain, which then makes scores (maybe *hundreds*) of increasingly finer corrections as the hand comes closer to the thing to be picked up. This happens far below your level of conscious awareness. In a mechanical sense, if it weren't for this cybernetic feedback from the brain, you and I would be covered from head to toe with scars from cuts, burns, and myriad other injuries—if we survived at all. As soon as your hand touches a hot stove your brain instantly fires a command to the muscles of your arm, which then jerks the hand away.

Under a microscope, a thin slice of brain tissue shows the same branching or dispersion principle employed by Nature in trees, lungs, and the arterial and venous blood systems. Like a cluster of flowers and weeds in a garden, each neuron extends tiny branches called dendrites which stretch outward to the dendrites of other neurons; this is how electrical messages are transmitted back and forth among these chains of neurons.

There are an estimated 13 million neurons in your body—10 million concentrated in the brain. Then there are about 4 million *special* neurons for the detection of pain, heat, cold, and to some extent, perhaps, the most sensitive of all psychophysical interactions, which we experience as love, fear, sexual stimulation, and so on.

The neurons of the organs and muscles are constantly sending messages to the brain about the position of the arms, the legs, hands, and feet; color perception; various smells; and minor aches and pains.

Each neuron has long, stalk-like fibers called axons which also carry messages to distant neurons like the wires that connect telephones in a local exchange. In a city or town, communication cables are made up of many telephone wires bundled together under the ground. A human nerve, analogous to the telephone cable, consists of a bundle of *thousands* of these axons.

The brain itself has no sensory organs. It can't feel. The skin, scalp and bones covering the skull however, can. Nature's profligacy in other areas is matched by her economy here. If a weapon or projectile smashes into a human head and penetrates the skin, scalp, or breaks the skull bones, there is good reason to be able to feel pain. If, however, the weapon crushes the skull and actually penetrates the brain, there's no logical reason for the organism to experience the warning signal of pain. If that happens, odds are that the body is already dead. Nature has "anticipated" such an eventuality.

A minor brain injury is called a concussion, which may or may not be serious. In addition to the protection given it by the skull, the brain is also protected by the cerebrospinal fluid which surrounds both the brain and spinal cord. This spinal cord is the main nerve center and carries the major load of messages back and forth to the brain. The liquid is something like the amniotic fluid surrounding the placenta prior to birth in that it protects the brain from sharp jolts and jarring.

When, in spite of this cerebrospinal fluid, the head receives a hard blow, it causes part of the brain to bump against the inside of the skull; the result—concussion.

There's a thin bony shelf inside the skull on which the main mass of the brain rests. This shelf has a hole through which runs the "stalk" or brainstem. In the middle there's a collection of countless millions of neurons, any of which is able to connect with nearby neurons in thousands of ways. This complex bundle of nerve tissue is called the reticular formation. "Reticular" means "like a net."

Modern brain researchers believe that the most important of all the brain's decisions are made in this area. Millions of messages per second arrive here from all over the body. In addition, the reticular formation also studies commands flashing in from other parts of the brain, and acts as a tiny kind of censor. It is so sensitive in this function that only a few hundred impulses out of *more than a hundred million electrical signals* are permitted to reach other parts of the brain. A few specialists suspect that because this enormous complex of neurons is so sensitive to drugs and tranquilizers (particularly hallucinogens like LSD, marijuana, and alcohol), it may rule consciousness and awareness.

During his highly publicized experiments, Canadian brain surgeon Dr. Wilder Penfield demonstrated that electrical stimulation of different areas of the exposed human brain reactivated memories so lifelike and vivid that his patients actually "relived" long-forgotten episodes of their lives.

The largest, most familiar part of the brain sits directly in back of the forehead. This is the cerebrum and is divided into the right and left hemispheres. The outer "skin" of the cerebrum is intricately convoluted. Each fold is almost an inch deep and contains thousands of millions of neurons. Nature's "decree" is that the cerebrum's convolutions take up a minimum of space inside the skull, otherwise our heads would be enormous. If it were possible to inflate the brain like a balloon, the creases would straighten smoothly, doubling the volume of our thinking organ.

Surprisingly, the amount of brain tissue in the cerebrum's motor and sensory areas has no relationship to the sizes of the sections of anatomy with which their neurons are connected. You have *more* feeling in your face and lips than in your abdomen, thighs, and chest and more control over your hands than all the rest of your body.

You don't actually "see" with your eyes. Their function is mainly to transpose incoming light into a complex series of electrical impulses. The actual "seeing" happens in the back part of the cerebrum where messages from the eyes arrive by way of the twin retinas and optic nerves. Located on each side of the cerebrum are the areas involved with—or controlling—speech and hearing.

Because the neurons on the right side of the cerebrum control the muscles of the left side of the body (and vice versa) this crossing-over of nerves *before* they reach the brain indicates that the structure of the brain is extremely more complex than anyone had previously believed.

Personality and intelligence was once believed to be controlled by the parts of the brain richest in neurons. The frontal areas of the brain are relatively quite large—considerably bigger than the same areas in the brains of monkeys, chimps, and gorillas, and rivaling those of dolphins, porpoises, elephants, and whales. Aside from this, almost nothing is known about the frontal section of the cerebrum, and to a lesser degree, certain parts of the sides and back. They are called the "silent areas" because they show no evidence of electrical activity. One exotic theory holds that these silent areas are used to exercise moral judgement—to determine "right" from "wrong."

Some evolutionists are convinced that they've found traces of the rudimentary brain of primitive creatures from which we are *supposed* to have evolved from life's early beginnings on Earth. They perceive this evidence in the four hollow spaces (the ventricles) hidden deeply within the base of the cerebrum. Below the ventricles a small mass of brain tissue called the thalamus is divided into two sections—or "lobes." This is believed to be a kind of primary "sorting office" for messages headed for the cerebrum. Brain experts consider the thalamus as the source of our general feeling of well-being and also of the first traces of discomfort or pain. Some physiologists actually believe that the human "biological clock" is located somewhere in the thalamus, but no clue to its physical shape or chemistry has ever been found.

The hypothalamus is a small mass of nerve tissue located just under the thalamus. It controls the pituitary gland which hangs like a tiny "stalk" from the thalamus. Because of its importance in governing the activity of the thyroid and other glands (particularly the secretion of sex hormones), the pituitary has the reputation of being the body's master gland.

The relationship of the pituitary gland to the hypothalamus causes some physiologists to think there is a cause-effect relationship between glandular disturbances and mental illnesses. The hypothalamus is at work when your heart pounds, your hands sweat, and your mouth is dry, for example. It also regulates sleep, hunger, and—you guessed it—your sex drive.

Most physiologists and anatomists are satisfied that they know how the brain is organized to control the whole spectrum of physical and mental activities, and yet the bothersome contradistinction between brain and Mind seems to be all but irreconcilable. Is man only a very sophisticated ape— a little further along the evolutionary ladder, say, than a monkey or dog?

Exactly what human characteristics are there that are not found in any other species?

A sense of humor for one. Laughter is uniquely human. It is difficult to define humor, yet life would be almost unbearable without it. It's a kind of appreciation or comprehension of the incongruous; humor requires balanced analytical judgement and intelligence. Animals are incapable of appreciating the incongruous; they simply can't comprehend humor.

Humans are also unique among animals in the capacity to appreciate beauty. A work of art, a beautiful creature, a sunset, or a great symphony may evoke an almost sensual appreciation in a human, while its essence would be completely lost to an animal.

Such appreciation of beauty requires a meditative state of mind—perception and quiet contemplation. Creative artistry demands a certain amount of concentration; distractions must be suppressed. Animals don't ordinarily look at pictures (although I have three cats that occasionally watch television and always roll over on command). No animal could comprehend a reason to deny the commands of its physical body in favor of a greater gain later on. Their brains don't seem to function in terms of past and future except to make crude comparisons based on attraction, fear, hunger, affection, and sex. Most creatures are totally incapable of planning ahead.

Only human beings recognize that beauty is derived from basic harmony, integrity, and order. *Man's attempt to impose moralistic strictures on himself is a reflection of the order found in the Universe.* A work of art is more than the sum of its parts—it's a spiritual and organic unity, an abstract integration privately perceived and intertwined with the individual psyche or subconscious. Emotional reactions to music can range from excitement or euphoria to sheer ecstasy. This is *Mind* at work, not brain. Horses, hyenas, and dogs don't seem to care for music.

Evolutionists often seem to be trying to create the impression that human consciousness is just quantitatively different from that of animals. The reason no animal can experience ecstasy (a spontaneous emotion of supreme exultation) is because it cannot transcend its physical sensations or its urge for immediate physical gratification.

Real thinking encompasses decision and planning, a kind of ongoing cybernetic reaction exceeding the capability of even the most intelligent animals. Ideally, aesthetic pleasure is infinitely superior to sensory stimulation, and only human beings have the capacity to appreciate it. But there are times when humans, suffering both mentally and emotionally, reject their higher consciousness and descend solely to the gratification of the physical senses—with predictable results.

A generation of hedonists notwithstanding, sexual morality

and continence seems to be a law of the Universe. It's no "coincidence" that only human beings can contract venereal diseases. Animals can't pick it up—not even from the diseased body of a human who has sunk to the level of bestiality. Our "social diseases" can be contracted only through careless or promiscuous behavior of the sort that pornography stimulates and encourages—sexual deviancy and orgiastic group sex with its variations.

The ready availability of drugs, coupled with the almost total rejection of legal restraints and the idea of self-discipline, may be signs that human history is repeating a cycle similar to the one that preceded the destruction of the biblical cities Sodom and Gomorrah. History may characterize the present era as another generation of vipers.

Only humans can experience the transcendant emotion of real ecstasy. Animals are conscious only on a limited scale—but not *self*-conscious, which is *the awareness of being conscious*. Animals cannot observe their own minds in action; only man can sense the influence of his higher self (or overriding soul) manipulating his mental processes.

Psychiatrist Erich Fromm says, "Man has intelligence, like other animals, which permits him to use thought processes for the attainment of immediate, practical aims; but man has another mental quality which the animal lacks. He is aware of himself, of his past and of his future, which is death; of his smallness and powerlessness; he is aware of others *as* others—as friends, enemies or strangers. Man transcends all other life because he is, for the first time, *life aware of itself*. Man is in nature, subject to its dictates and accidents, yet he transcends Nature because he lacks the unawareness which makes the animal a part of Nature—as one with it."

Also in *Life—The Unfinished Experiment* (1974's National Book Award winner), Nobel laureate Salvadore E. Luria observed that "Life is different from all other natural phenomena in one feature: it has a program ... Stupendous devices such as the brain and mind of man are biochemical inventions as challenging and as mysterious as those that produced the equally stupendous social organization of insects. To the scientist, the uniqueness of man is purely a biological uniqueness rather than the superposition of something nonbiological—soul or spiritual essence—upon the workings of biological evolution. The nature of the mechanisms responsible for these highly complex phenomena still escapes the biologist, but he is confident that this will not always be so."*

Was there ever an *"evolution* of consciousness?" or was it created just as the dramatic imagery of the biblical Genesis implies? In either case, Homo sapiens appears to be evolving; *the creation of Genus Terran* seems to be Nature's current aim—a totally new species of genus *Homo*—spacefaring man. In *Man: The Bridge Between Two Worlds,*† Franz E. Winkler, M.D. states, "The story of man himself, of his spirit, cannot be told in intellectual terms; it requires the universal language of art, which speaks to the heart itself. Intuitive experiences can never be adequately expressed in words. However, the magnificent imagery of legends, myths, and true folklore can arouse in all men— as they have in the past—a divination of the absolute."

The transcendental human reaction of ecstasy to great musical art is a reflection of mathematics (as was indicated by the Pythagoraean music of the spheres). Materialistic scientists have long pondered the question of whether mathematics is an invention of the mind or if it exists as part of the real Universe. Since the human brain (and/or Mind) appears to be a product of the Real Universe, the answer may be *both*.

The late Jesuit anthropologist, Pierre Teilhard de Chardin once observed that "The great superiority we have acquired over the animals and even Primitive Man (and which will be enhanced by our descendants in a degree perhaps undreamed-of by ourselves) is in the realm of self-knowledge; in our growing capacity to situate ourselves in space and time, to the point of becoming *conscious of our place and responsibility in relation to the Universe* . . . we are beginning to realise that our nobility consists in serving, like intelligent atoms, the work proceeding in the Universe. We have discovered

*S. E. Luria, *Life—The Unfinished Experiment*, Scribner's, New York, 1973.

†Franz E. Winkler, *Man: The Bridge Between Two Worlds*, Harper, New York, 1960.

that there is a Whole, of which we are the elements. We have found the world in our own souls."

He describes the coming process of *superpersonalization*, or the evolution of Homo sapiens, through self-knowledge, into a higher, more refined, and infinitely greater species of being: "Imagine men awakening at last, under the influence of the ever-tightening planetary embrace, to a sense of universal solidarity based on their profound community, evolutionary in its nature and Purpose. The nightmares of brutalisation and mechanisation which are conjured up to terrify us and prevent our advance are at once dispelled. It is not harshness or hatred but a new kind of love, *not yet experienced by man*, which we must learn to look for as it is borne to us on the rising tide of planetisation (of the species)."

Is this then, the "preparation" the human race must undergo in order to be worthy of experiencing or participating in an infinitely higher form of emotion than anything previously known or imagined? *The love of one species of intelligent beings for another?*

Teilhard suggested this in his description of man's arrival at the *supreme synthesis.* "If journeying between celestial bodies were practicable, it is hard to see why we ourselves have not already been invaded ... Mankind, at the end of its totalisation, may reach a critical level of maturity where, leaving Earth (the species) will detach itself from this planet and join the one true, irreversible essence of things, *the Omega point.*"

In the progression of Genus Terran we are being *forced* to look backward—to learn by hard experience that we are struggling to free our natures *from* animalism in order to be able to perceive the reality of our existence as higher octave forms of energy.

The closest human example of the way an animal "thinks" or "feels" as it follows its natural instincts is in the manner of a man (who is either drugged, hypnotized, or sleep-deprived and exhausted) trying to perform a simple task at someone else's command. According to biologist Theodosius Bobzhansky: "Self-awareness, or conscious awareness, or Mind, is by far the most important of the characteristics which make man human, and yet is also by far the most difficult one to study scientifically."

Even with the birth of the new science of genetics in the early 1960s and the discovery of the DNA and RNA molecules, the true essence of man escaped materialistic science, which even now seems only dimly aware of the great potential of field physics.

Anthropologist Dwight Bidney is in agreement with Teilhard de Chardin: "Man is a self-reflecting animal in that he alone has the ability to objectify himself, to stand apart from himself, as it were, and to consider the kind of Being he is, and what it is that he wants to do and to become. Other animals may be conscious of their affects and the objects perceived; man alone is capable of reflection or self-consciousness, of thinking of himself as an object . . ."

Science has long regarded "Mind" as a kind of four-letter word to be avoided at all costs by the "well-bred" materialist. Here is how Dr. Bidney addressed himself to this attitude: "No matter how eloquently somebody may argue that my self-awareness is just an illusion, I know, with an assurance greater than I have about anything else in the world, that my self-awareness is *the most compelling of all realities.*"

The objective of human evolution according to Teilhard, is the planetization of our species. We are the *stewards* of this Earth, which like all other planets in the solar system, is composed of two distinctly different hemispheres (are the brain's two halves symbolic of this?), the discovery of which poses still another scientific riddle. Part of our responsibility as planetary stewards is to protect and preserve the Earth's myriad life forms and to understand our relationship to them, and in the process perhaps to understand something of the relationship of man to his Creator. This urge is evidenced by the enthusiasm for books and documentary films about nature and wildlife. In *Science News* for November 30, 1974, René Dubos wrote, "*The unique place of our species in the order of things is determined not by its animality but by its humanity.*"

Another of the characteristic differences between humans and animals is in their attitude toward death and the disposal of their dead. Animals have few or none; no species of animal has even the crudest sort of death ceremonial; they don't even bury their dead. Ants, despite their great social sophistication, simply throw their dead out of their nests along with other trash. Some animals practice cannibalism; demented female monkeys have been known to cling stubbornly to the bodies of their dead (sometimes decomposed) infants. Among the animals man is alone in recognizing the inevitability of death, the desirability of making preparations for it and engaging in ritual ceremonials afterward.

This ability we have to think in abstract terms of the future is in sharp contradistinction to the limited time sense of even the most intelligent primates. In order to climb a tree with the idea of picking, peeling, and eating a piece of fruit, a relatively intelligent chimpanzee must strain its mental abilities to their limit. The animal brain is incapable of thinking in the dimension of time except in relation to itself; at that, it is severely limited.

Through his language, man can denote and specify the past and the future beyond the span of his own life. Ethnologist W. H. Thorpe made the following observation about abstract thinking: "Man can internalize relations perceived in the external world to a vastly greater extent than the animals. In other words, man can manipulate completely abstract symbols to an extent far beyond that possible in the animal world ... no animal language, no matter how much information is conveyed, involves the learned realization of completely general abstractions."

And Dostoyevski wrote, "Man needs the unfathomable and the infinite just as much as he does the small planet which he inhabits."

Blaise Pascal, the seventeenth-century philosopher, wondered, "When I consider the short duration of my life, swallowed up in the eternity before and after, the little space which I fill and even can see, engulfed in the infinite immensity of spaces of which I am ignorant and which know me not, I am frightened and astonished at being here rather than there, why now rather than then? Who has put me here? By whose order and direction have this place and time been allotted to me?"

Psychologist and linguist expert Eric H. Lenneberg said,

"... humans also construct and identify the relationships between symbolic sounds. In other words, humans understand sentence structure—syntax and the *connection* between words. Whether the brain of a chimpanzee has the same or similar properties must yet be demonstrated. It is possible but not probable."*

Intensive studies have been made of the "languages" of creatures such as termites, ants, bees, chimpanzees, dolphins, and whales. But according to Frank McMullin, these communications differ sharply from the languages of human beings in that they are "species specific, inherited, not learnt. Their use is instinctive, not reflective. Honey bees of one species will not be able to 'follow' the language of another species nor can they learn it. Genetic differences can even arise within species due to geographic separation; an Italian honeybee cannot follow the cues given by a hive of its German cousins. Once an Italian honeybee, always an Italian honeybee."

Whatever animal languages there are in existence tend to stagnate, while human languages are dynamically alive and adaptable. "Man does not inherit a language," McMullin emphasized, "he has no endowment of language signs ... human languages have to be learnt ... To the child, they come extra-ordinarily easily and quickly; for the adult, it may require a great effort to acquire a new language. But just because they are not programmed into the human brain, man's languages possess a feature that more than compensates for the effort it takes to learn them. They are capable of being modified at will, to respond to new kinds of situations. There is a *creative* element here, an implicit demand on human creativity that is seldom recognized."

All animals make sounds of one kind or another, which is why speech researchers are baffled over the inability of animals to develop the capacity of vocal language. The monkeys' screeches and gestures will warn others that a predator is near, but none have ever learned to tell the difference between "snake," "leopard," "lion," or "fire."

Man is also unique in his capacity for historical communication—an extension of speech—the ability to pass on to the

*It has since been proven to be both.

next generation the the accumulated knowledge of past generations, provided, of course, that there have been no catastrophic interruptions in the course of history. This talent implies a purposeful evolutionary intent. Until the present time the lessons of history which we've passed on to each succeeding generation seem to have been generally lost, or if not lost then tinted with the irrationalities, prejudices, superstitions, and fears of the past.

The evolution of Genus Terran as a planetary species—the ever-changing culture of human society—is dramatically different from the relative "stagnancy" of animal society. On the other hand, it may be that Homo sapiens isn't all that unique in the cosmos. Perhaps there are great civilizations spread across the Galaxy (and beyond) composed of undreamed-of variations of the genus Homo. While we discover more about the human family and the riddles of evolution, and as the mystery surrounding man's true origins are increasingly complicated, the clearer it becomes that other species of (quite possibly) nonhuman intelligent, rational beings have evolved equally complex brains and languages. There are undoubtedly great alien cultures of nonhuman civilizations somewhere in space. If this is as likely as it seems, then it's even more likely that representatives of those civilizations could have visited the Earth at any time (perhaps during our "prehistoric" periods) and left artifacts or some other trace of their presence. This theory is now regarded as scientifically plausible.

Technology stands at the crudest, most cumbersome era of space travel. Our mighty cannibalistic rockets, fueled by millions of tons of costly chemicals, are the "gas bags" of space voyaging. Compared to the fantastic vessels of the future, today's powerful boosters are the equivalent of the Montgolfier brothers' hot-air-inflated linen bag, or to the Wright brothers' stick-and-cloth prototype of the airplane.

Ever since American astronauts began to leave traces of their presence on the Moon—and Soviet and American space probes started parachuting sensors into the atmospheres of Venus, Mars, and Jupiter—it has become easier for us to understand how the same events could—and quite possibly did—happen eons ago.

And yet, Dr. Carl Sagan, director of Cornell University's Planetary Sciences Department and probably America's foremost expert on the solar system, planetary atmospheres, and life and intelligence on other worlds, wryly commented that "Life, consciousness and intelligence have most probably evolved among other solar systems, but almost certainly there are no *men* anywhere else in the Universe. Even if evolution were to begin all over again right here on the Earth—with the identical ingredients and the same random factors such as mutations by cosmic radiation and so forth, we'd wind up with *nothing* resembling man!" (Sagan is an ardent Darwinian evolutionist.)

It begins to look suspiciously as though we're intimately involved in a Grand Design which we're only dimly aware of. The pieces are beginning to fit however, and the clearer it seems that we are destined to explore and colonize the planets and then the stars.

Stupendous as it seems, such an adventure may be as common an event in each Galaxy as are hundreds of thousands of graduating classes on all educational levels throughout the world. If the "schedule" is kept, we will witness the withering and gradual elimination of competition and war as tools of international diplomacy, and the appreciation of man as a unique entity in the Galaxy.

Aside from conquering disease and increasing our knowledge, power, and the ability to bring human reproduction into balance with Earth's resources, the major nations of our planet are desperately engaged in hammering out treaties to avoid a nuclear holocaust that might forever extinguish all trace of man in the universe. We possess this capability—*plus* the freedom to choose either course. Either we accept fully the responsibilities of stewardship of our fragile, delicately balanced planet or we do not.

Are we prepared for the "final examination" before "graduation" from this planetary grammar school?

If we are to make it, it's imperative that we gain total control over the animalistic promptings of the right brain and stifle its negative biological emotions—fear, greed, and superstition—and begin to live in a spirit of mutual trust, cooperation, and love.

The most noble of all human urges is to curb hostility, competition, and greed and to generate a truly humanistic concern and compassion for all creatures. The options are minimal—either we make it or we don't. The choice— possibly for the first time in recorded history—is entirely our own. Other human cultures composed of our most dimly re- mote ancestors may have failed the same tests we now face. The acceptance of responsibility (and the value we place on the symbiosis of the planetary ecology) may help to deter- mine our fitness for the next evolutionary step.

Why, at this juncture of history, the emphasis on preserv- ing vanishing species and appreciating the diffusion and mag- nificence of other terrestrial forms? Is it to remind us that there are alternative forms as vessels for consciousness and intelligence? In the past, man's obvious superiority to the ani- mals generated a kind of contempt for them. This is chang- ing. We're beginning to realize the almost irreparable loss in such cruel and barbaric practices as hunting and killing inno- cent creatures for pleasure or mercilessly trapping and tortur- ing harmless animals whose sole "offense" is being beautiful, thus stimulating human greed for possession of their beautiful pelts. What excuse is there now for fashionable, wealthy women to wear the skins of slaughtered leopards, ermine, or fox at a time when technology can closely duplicate such materials—often at less expense than the originals?

(*And what if the citizens of another solar system turn out to be a race of superintelligent ocelots?*)

A new respect almost bordering on love for all life is stir- ring the Mass Consciousness. More than ever before, nations are striving to halt such practices as the annual slaughter of scores of thousands of whales, the world's largest and most magnificent animal. At the same time we are gradually awak- ening to the realization that while *something* unique charac- terizes us from other species, from all other life forms, it doesn't completely isolate us from other species.

Genus Terran's attitudes, relationships, and behavior toward life (regardless of its form or function) will surely be diametrically opposed to yesterday's ruthless exploitation by Homo sapiens.

We're learning.

Chapter Nine

Psionics, Acupuncture and Genetics

A quasi-electronic device located at a distance from the organisms it was radionically treating caused a series of genetic crossings among different varieties of the same species. The Life Fields of these plants and trees, apparently, were *merged* psionically—their genes and chromosomes mixed—to produce totally new varieties of hybrid trees and fruit!

And in spite of the progress made in the long study of genetics, orthodox scientists are having grave misgivings over some of the "diabolical" experiments now in progress in many laboratories. Molecular biologists have overcome Nature's "immune reaction" in certain plant and animal cells and have already wide-crossed the cells of human beings with those of mice, rats, *and even insects!*

On a spring afternoon in 1972 while I was examining a radionic device for medical diagnosis and treatment at the home of Arthur Young, president of the Foundation for the Study of Consciousness, he told me an unusual story:

One of his friends who had been plagued by insects infesting six or seven trees on his land decided to try an adaptation of the Hieronymus Machine to get rid of the pests. He placed a photograph of those trees in his device, and without using any reagent or repellent, *concentrated* on driving the insects away. As he rotated the dial, he detected a difference in the feel of the plate he was stroking, so he fixed the dial at that setting and returned to an unfinished job in his barn.

A few hours later while he was totally absorbed in the work and not thinking about anything in particular, thousands of starlings, grackles, and cowbirds descended from the clear skies shrieking an untranslatable cacophony, and covered every branch of every tree in the photograph. Within an hour the birds had eaten all the insects and departed.

"If that was just a coincidence," said Arthur Young, "the odds against it were astronomical. Is there an energy field or medium through which Mind itself can perceive and influence other life forms? Did his thoughts as he turned the dial and stroked the plate of the psionic device form 'signals' that called the birds to their feast of insects?"

Some researchers in radionics think so.

In Harrisburg, Pennsylvania, one-time headquarters of General Gross' Homeotronic Research Foundation, the elm trees along Front Street in the Keystone state's capital were severely afflicted by the Dutch elm disease. General Gross tried unsuccessfully to interest incredulous city officials in a demonstration of psionic control of the spreading disease. The retired general handed a series of aerial photographs of the trees (taken from a helicopter) to another psionics experimenter, Muriel Benjamin of New Cumberland. She "treated" the trees without compensation and in less than a month the Dutch elm disease in the area was nonexistent.

"We're constantly learning something new," Mrs. Benjamin said, referring to the way she and her husband, Roland, use psionic control on their trees. "I've always used a crystal of tungsten nickle fluoride to stimulate the growth of plants and trees, but when our trees had the apple scab disease, Galen and Louise Hieronymus came up with oxbile tablets as a reagent and cleared up the disease among the trees down by our smokehouse. I passed this information on to other experimenters, and it worked for some of them, but not all. I often wonder if tungsten nickle fluoride works for me because I *believe* in it?"

"There's no concerted research being done," General Gross said during this meeting in 1972. "We're often working in the dark and have to be very careful. Almost anything can happen and we can't always undo what we've started."

"That's true," said Muriel Benjamin. "Nobody is smarter than Nature. For years we've used nicotine sulfate as a reagent to stop the spread of the spruce budworm—actually spruce gall. One of the cases I treated was at Silver Lake. In order to keep the larvae from spreading in the early spring I placed a bottle of nicotine sulfate on the collector plate with a photograph of the trees to be treated* and it did the job very nicely."

In 1953 when the Dutch elm disease was spreading in Washington, D.C., Mrs. Benjamin asked a friend to take a series of pictures of the affected trees along Pennsylvania Avenue from the top of the Washington Monument. She began her psionic treatment of the trees as soon as the photographs arrived in the mail. Within six months the Dutch elm disease in the nation's capital was gone. Psionics however, didn't get the credit.

In another experiment—this time overseas—her U.K.A.C.O. radionics box nearly saved the economy of an emerging African nation. "When Ghana seemed about to make it as a republic," Muriel Benjamin related, "their secretary of agriculture and one of his assistants were in Canada when they heard about the work we were doing, so they called and arranged to visit us on their way home.

"Over dinner one night they asked if we would try to save their cacao trees from a spreading insect blight. From the export of the cacao bean from which cocoa and chocolate are made, these trees are a major source of Ghana's revenue.

"After they returned to Ghana they sent back detailed photographs and the most exacting maps, which gave the precise locations and altitudes of their major cacao-growing areas. I started experimenting with different reagents and within a few weeks learned that the treated areas were being cured of the blight. This was in 1952 before popular elections. But as soon as Kwame Nkrumah became prime minister he grabbed control over everything and started jailing his political rivals without trial. That was the last I heard of the secretary of agriculture, and from then on Ghana's blighted cacao crop dropped to a fraction of its former volume."

Like many psionics experimenters, Mrs. Benjamin is keenly interested in genetics. "Every living thing is completely unique," she told me. "None of us are very much like our parents—or our children either. We're all the result of every conceivable genetic combination since the beginning."

*The photograph and the nicotine sulfate are placed together on the "sensor" which extends by a wire from the radionic device.

(This straightforward, charming, and intelligent woman may accidentally have made the most important and exciting discovery in the history of radionics.) "I don't concentrate during my plant treatment periods," she confessed. "Oftentimes I'll be doing something entirely different while the machine is on—treating crops or trees almost anywhere. I've made my share of mistakes too, but the worst blunder of all was with four different varieties of peach trees Roland and I planted here. I took four photographs—one of each of those trees—and alternately treated them to stimulate their growth and yield. For two years it worked beautifully. I placed one photo in an envelope at a time on the collector plate and laid a crystal of calcite or tungsten nickle fluoride on it for a few hours each day. Well, about the third year I got rushed, so to save time, I 'ran' all the negatives together with the calcite crystal.

"The next year there was a terrible mess. First, the latest-blooming tree blossomed first and the early one last. The others were a mishmosh of inedible, useless fruit. Everything was either too small, too hard, too mushy, without seeds, or rotten. There were dozens of different varieties of peaches on each tree. It was such a mess of nothing that we were eventually forced to take all four trees out of the ground. By placing the pictures all together the way I did, the machine had somehow garbled their genetic codes. Somewhere back in their cross-bred ancestry I had scrambled their genes.

"We just couldn't believe it at first, so we let them grow for another year just to be sure."

It wasn't an isolated case. "Curtis Upton (another psionics experimenter) once took a 'sourceless key' (*a carbonized image of the tree's bark*) from an English walnut tree, and once he had separated it, used the key on a black walnut tree. In effect, he cross-bred it. From then on, we were getting *very* large walnuts, but they were tan like English walnuts, and the shells were easily separated. They almost fell apart.

"My mistake with the peach trees was in using the *negatives* which I placed *face down* on the collector plate, glossy side up. Then I laid the calcite crystal on top. I don't know how it worked, but I think it must have blended the vital fields of those trees to cross their genes that way."

Incredible? Sure it is. But so were the first X-ray pictures of the interior of the human body. Scientists have since learned that these invisible radiations can alter chromosome structure and genes, thus influencing or changing heredity. It may be that hard radiation and electromagnetism *affect the L-fields* of living things—bacteria, animals, trees, and humans. Directly or indirectly, magnetism and electricity also have a powerful effect on organic systems. The burgeoning science of biomagnetic healing proves that wound-healing, bone-mending—even psychological well-being—are accelerated and enhanced by exposure to electromagnetic fields.

It may be that these fields do *not* have a direct physical effect. They may augment or strengthen the healing energy of the L-field, which in some mysterious way—perhaps through the body's vital points—*directly* controls the entire organism.

Electroshock therapy, for example, has long been used in the treatment of severe depression. Shocking the brain and central nervous system with electricity does have an immediate and direct physical effect. The controlling L-field (including the grandular and nervous systems and the brain) is influenced by electricity and magnetism. Any change in personality after strong electroshock, therefore, may also be attributed to changes in the flow of energy from the L-field. Biomagnetic healing, acupuncture, and shock therapy probably work through their influence on the L-field. Mind also affects the body's controlling field of energy.

The ancient Chinese art of acupuncture postulates 900 points of radiant energy strategically located on the body. Each point correlates to a physical organ and may well be energy transfer junctures where the L-field interacts with the body. At New York University's Department of Anesthesiology, Dr Frank Warren embarked on a five-year study in which severely disturbed mental patients are being treated with acupuncture.

"This will cut down or eliminate the use of shock therapy. It could also decrease the need for long-term incarceration of the criminally insane," he said. All the patients in his group had previously undergone orthodox medical and psychiatric treatment—*without success.*

"I insert two needles—one in each ear near the auditory

145

canal, the traditional Chinese acupuncture points," Dr. Warren explained. The results of this study, which began in 1972, have been extremely promising and offer great hope. "The needles are inserted two or three times a week for the first few months and once a week thereafter," he said. Dr. Lewis Wolberg, medical director of New York's Postgraduate Center for Mental Health, where the acupuncture study originated, describes Warren as "one of the foremost acupuncturists in the century."

As Drs. Burr, Ravitz, and Langman repeatedly demonstrated, the L-field is the matrix-forming field of energy that controls the shape and function of the body. Exactly how electricity, acupuncture, and magnetism influence this nonphysical field of energy remains a mystery.

What, for example, is the "mechanism" for locating, identifying, or "treating" someone (radionically) from a blood sample, a lock of hair, or skin scraping? This is an area where genetic biologists and radionic/psionic researchers are in general agreement. The theory of most pioneers in the field is that every living thing—in fact every organ, cell, molecule, and atom—constantly broadcasts on its own characteristic wavelength. A living cell or tissue radiates its harmonious relationship to its parent organ and also acts as its "resonant point of contact"—even from great distances. Thus, a sample of a patient's blood enables the operator of a psionics device to locate, diagnose, or "treat" the patient, even if they happen to be separated by thousands of miles. Barriers are no obstacle, and the inverse-square law doesn't seem to apply.

For some reason or other, orthodox science is closer to accepting this heterodox theory than ever before. Cornelius G. McWright, head of the FBI's biological research unit, is now using an electrophoretic method to "fingerprint" blood samples more specifically. Forensic researchers feel they're on the brink of determining sex from a small spot of fresh or dried blood, a strand of hair or a skin scraping. "In fresh blood," McWright said late in December 1974, "there's a nuclear appendage (a small chromosome-containing body in the nucleus of the white blood cell) which indicates a female donor. Staining the blood sample will show up the male Y-chromosome. But the best approach," he said, "is the use of *radio* assay to identify hormones which are present in different ratios in the blood of men and women."

The challenge of forensic science is drawing it closer to psionics. From a single strand of hair many different characteristics can now be determined: race, the place of origin of the body, whether the hair was bleached, whether it fell out naturally or was cut, crushed, pulled, or burned. Exact blood types can be determined from a hair or from male semen. The scientific sleuths will soon be able to determine sex from a strand of hair (because the chromatin of sex is found in the root).

In chemistry and biology, according to Cecil E. Yates, Jr., chief of the FBI's chemical research unit, "It's beginning to look as though all living things have a closer relationship than anyone had previously suspected."

Despite this interrelationship, biochemists were still baffled by the biological forces that prevented one species from mating with another. Until recently, this was one of the greatest obstacles against organ transplants. A number of different drugs that suppress the body's ability to reject an organ transplant have since been developed. Dr. Lynn S. Bates of Kansas State University used some of these drugs in horticultural experiments to determine whether the long-cherished dream of plant breeders is possible—to combine the most desirable characteristics from completely different agricultural crops into a single "superplant."

Cross-fertilization between two varieties of the *same* species is normally accomplished by removing the male organs from the androgynous (bisexual or hermaphroditic) flowers of the plant. This prevents the plant from pollinating itself. Pollen from a *different* variety (of the same species) is then dusted over the remaining female organs.

But if the two varieties belong to *different species*, the pollen won't fertilize the ova of the female organs. This is somewhat analogous to the immune mechanism among animals in which the host will reject a graft of foreign tissue.

The International Corn and Wheat Improvement Center at El Batan, Mexico, is trying to develop a series of tough, hardy plants to resist insects, survive droughts, and still produce extra large yields of highly nutritious food. They have already been successful in creating strange species of food plants that may be the forerunners of new and different crops in the future.

Working in close cooperation with Dr. Bates is Mexico's Dr. Armando Campos, who has developed plants that combine the drought and disease resistance of barley, the self-fertilizing root system of the soybean, and the high yield and food value of wheat—all different species.

For a period of several days Dr. Bates had injected barrier-neutralizing drugs into the leaf enclosing a wheat spike as its flowers emerged. When he dusted the female wheat organs with pollen from a barley plant, fertilization was accomplished and an entirely new kind of plant—an embryonic but long-sought superplant—was finally created.

In a way, his success is even more significant than Muriel Benjamin's accidental radionic scrambling of her peach tree's genes. She took the sensible precaution of having the hybrids uprooted and destroyed. She didn't repeat the experiment for fear that such genetic tampering could have dangerous long-range effects. (*Biologists and horticulturists are convinced that today's balanced diversity of plant and animal species never could have evolved as distinct lineages without the biological barrier that has prevented interbreeding among different species. But this may not always have been so, as we'll soon see.*)

The "immune barrier" in plants was neutralized by a chemical called colchicine. Dr. Campos adapted and improved the techniques developed by Dr. Bates and is now growing a variety of "wide-crossed" (i.e., from different species) seeds into adult plants. As these techniques are perfected, an ever-growing number of wide crosses are surviving —wheat with barley, barley with rye, wheat with rye, wheat and a wild grass, corn and a wild, corn-like species that is resistant to drought, and many others.

At first the new plants were often sterile; they carried a set of chromosomes from one species with a *nonmatching* set from another. But Dr. Campos also solved this problem with colchicine, and now the chromosomes in each cell are able to duplicate themselves. As a result, all the cells of the hybridized plants have been given matching sets of chromosomes.

This makes them fertile and—through self-pollination—able to produce their own new generation of fertile seeds.

Of course this Frankensteinian tampering is only with plants. It's just a matter of time, however, before similar methods are attempted in the genetic manipulation of higher organisms, including human beings. According to Gordon R. Taylor in *The Biological Time Bomb* (New American Library) that time may already be upon us. "The breakthrough has already been made," he claims. "We're now in the opening stages of a biological revolution of greater impact than our industrial and technological revolutions. The possibilities are as frightening as the breakthroughs in nuclear fusion and fission."

Or worse; he's being too conservative. Sooner or later human embryos will be brought to life in the laboratory. Scientists can now take a carrot cell, for example, and from it grow exact copies of the original carrot. The next attempts will probably be made with exact copies of thoroughbred horses, pedigree dogs and cats, prize bulls, and—if the controlling Fields of Life are somehow bypassed or overcome—it will be tried with human beings.

To Gordon Taylor, such prospects are horrifying. "The most staggering possibilities are man's imminent power to interfere in the process of heredity, to alter the genetic structures of his own species," he says. If successful, such tampering could lead to anything from gene warfare to the creation of completely new types of living creatures—"fish men" to live in the oceans, strange beings able to breathe the rarefied atmosphere of Mars, quasihuman monsters to live in the crushing gravity fields and noxious atmospheres of gigantic Jupiter and Saturn.

Are such things really possible? They may seem like a devil's nightmare now, but life often has a tendency to surpass the wildest fiction. Biochemists at the Stanford University Medical School and the U.C. Medical Center in San Francisco are into genetic engineering up to their chromosomes. In 1973 they developed a practical method of transplanting genes from the complex cells of animals into the very simple but fast-multiplying cells of bacteria. Their aim was to develop specific stretches of the genetic chemical

DNA (deoxyribonucleic acid) into bacterial "factories" so that biochemists like Stanford's Nobel Prize winner Dr. Joshua Lederberg can determine "just how animal genes are turned on and off."

It may sound innocuous, but an alarm has been sounded by deeply concerned American scientists who have demanded a global moratorium on genetic engineering. At a recent international symposium organized by the Gottleib Duttweiler Institute in Dayos, Switzerland, scientists clashed head-on. Although the majority recognized the "terrible danger of unbridled genetic tampering," they were convinced that any effort to set up controls would be "impractical and unenforceable."

A representative of the Swedish Institute for Medical Research and Genetics, for instance, reported having successfully crossed the genes of entirely different genera and families to produce living hybrid cells. His team had actually combined human cells with the chromosomes of rats, mice, chick embryos—and *insects!* "We've now successfully produced 'man-mouse' cells and even stranger combinations," said Dr. Nils Ringertz.

What will happen if men like Dr. Ringertz gain control over human evolution? If the controlling L-field is somehow overriden or bypassed, those "man-mouse" and "man-insect" cells could eventually be grown into mature grotesqueries. As indicated in a previous chapter, civilization and science may have reached astonishing degrees of advancement many times in the ancient past. The great cereal grains, corn, wheat, rice, and barley were once little more than wild grass-like plants. Yet they've been standard agricultural crops for more than 10,000 years, living proof that genetics and crossbreeding were known to ancient people.

Horses, cattle, and other domestic animals also may have been genetically altered. The speared narwhal is a curious kind of whale, and still exists. Many creatures are extinct but, what about unicorns, centaurs, and mermaids? Were they just flights of human fancy, or did such creatures once exist? If today's genetic engineers can combine cells of rats and insects with human cells, their ancient counterparts may have gone even farther afield and crossed human genes with those of a goat to produce a satyr. Where did the ideas for the sphynx, the gargoyle, and phoenix originate? What about the cyclops, the hydra, or any of the bizarre creatures in ancient mythology?

Even if the overriding Fields of Life *don't allow* the genetic crossing of human cells with those of beasts, grave dangers still remain. .... *planetwide epidemics, for example.*

Dr. Paul Berg, head of the biochemistry department of Stanford University (*himself a pioneer in building interspecies hybrid chromosomes*) formally renounced his own work as being extremely dangerous early in 1974. By midsummer he was heading a group backed by the National Academy of Sciences that called for an international moratorium on genetic tampering—at least until controls are developed. The two avenues of research he most fears are the cultivation of new bacteria which are immune to all antibiotics, and the linkage of DNA molecules with viruses that could cause widespread cancers.

"Several groups of scientists are already using this technology," he warned. "Such experiments can result in the creation of totally new, unpredictably infectious, and deadly viruses. If they ever escape from the laboratory, God help us. These new infections would spread widely and quickly among humans, and there would be no defense against them."

Under such conditions there would be global epidemics of such fearsome virulence that they would wipe out most of the human race and possibly every other species as well.

In March 1975, at Asilomar, California, an international conference of molecular biologists (including Soviet and Chinese representatives) reported that thousands of laboratories throughout the world are now engaged in genetic experiments. "Many of these are so hazardous," said Dr. Berg, "that they should never have been undertaken. Scientists have constructed totally new kinds of chromosomes *that do not exist in Nature.* Containing and controlling them is a deadly serious problem."

If genetics *was* practiced in ancient times, there could have been horned horses (unicorns) and even stranger creatures, but they would probably have been sterile.

Max Birnstiel of the Zurich Institute for Molecular Biology

151

wants no lines drawn. "The potential benefits of genetic manipulation are so great that this sort of research is gaining uncontrollable momentum. I personally consider that we are just now at the very brink of a great information explosion ... on the interaction of genetic units in higher organisms."

Basel University Microbiological Center's Dr. Werber Arber openly criticized those who would curb such work. "No one should hamper basic science for any reason," he said. "Genetic research can't be stopped."

Possibly not, but it should be slowed down.

At the University of Maryland, scientists have developed a new breed of naked chicken; a rare mutation that looks like a living preplucked broiler. "I don't think they're aware of the fact that they're naked, said Dr. Max Rubin, a research associate in the poultry-science department. "They cut and bruise easily and lack a normal bird's sense of balance, but the meat looks and tastes the same as the normal barnyard pullet's flesh."

The odds of hatching a freak featherless chick by chance alone is one in several billions. The hybrids lack a protective coat of feathers and must be kept in coops with very high temperatures. This raises the cost of heating and as a result their commercial value is limited. Other interesting genetic experiments are also underway to increase the tenderness and yield of cattle beef by creating new species of domestic animals.

But the most insidious of all immediate prospects, according to Stanford's Dr. Paul Berg, is a movement to enforce prenatal detection tests to enforce compulsory abortion for fetuses with genetic defects. "For parents who already have a defective child and might be at definite risk of having another," said Yale University geneticist Dr. Y. Edward Hsia, "appropriate preventative treatment is in order—that is, *enforced birth control*. Of course, I could condone such measures only as a last resort if vulnerable couples or mothers refused to comply on a voluntary basis.

"If such a mother or family should choose to ignore the risk and continue to procreate, the cost to society will be multiplied by the birth of each affected individual. In such a situation, society should take upon itself the right to limit the number of children such a family might bear. When society is forced to shoulder the medical and social cost of caring for individuals with inherited genetic defects, the right to procreation should and must be restricted.

"This is a public health problem. The community has every right to restrict the movements of someone with a highly contagious disease, so why not genetic diseases as well? They aren't contagious, but they are transmissible."

Dr. Charles Hine of UC-San Francisco echoed his argument. "A new world—in which certain personal liberties will have to disappear—is being born," he said.

In view of the overriding "authority" of the Fields of Life over chromosomes and genes, including the DNA and RNA molecules that supposedly have the last word on heredity, widespread genetic tampering may prove to be impossible. The latest information gained about the organizing, intangible L-field is that it can be modified—and often overridden—*by the even less tangible power of human thought*. This helps to explain why terminal cancer patients have cured themselves through meditation. But it doesn't explain how—by using only a sample of blood as a *"point of contact"*—patients have been located and treated across great distances.

Can there be, as Dr. Harold S. Burr claimed, a genetic relationship between trees and human beings? Biochemists interested in wide-crossing the genes of different families of living things recently stumbled on an amazing discovery in support of such an extraordinary relationship: they found that *when an atom of magnesium is detached from a chlorophyll molecule and an atom of iron put in its place it becomes a molecule of red blood!*

Psionics researchers believe that mind can also effect such a change because radionics influences living organisms through their L-fields. In *The Future of Radionics*,* Clarence Winchester wrote, "Through the practice of radionics it is possible for anyone to be diagnosed at a distance by rapport and receive treatment by return. His state of health can be monitored by this method rather like a form of 'psychological radar.' If a certain form of energy is sent to him he will be

*"Mind & Matter," Delawarr Laboratories, Dec. 1966.

stimulated accordingly. This is the basis of a new science which enables its practitioners to treat animals and crops in the same way."

In the early 1950s The Radionic Centre Organisation was formed at Oxford, England. *Its aims*:

"1) To seek a greater knowledge of what constitutes mind and to promote research in this field.

"2) To study the effect of thought energy on living tissue.

"3) To promote the advancement of knowledge in relation to the science of radionics in all its aspects, and to provide a center for people who want to study the subject.

"4) To provide a meeting ground for those who wish to become proficient in radionics in order to render service to human beings and animals, or its application to agriculture.

"5) To provide a meeting ground for scientists to study the laws of the primary state of matter, as embraced by radionics, giving special attention to the behavior of magnetism and gravity in the prephysical state before the atom forms.

"6) To integrate religion, science and philosophy, using the study of the power of thought as a common denominator.

"7) To study the transmission of energy as in radionic therapy; and

"8) To consider the possibility of transmitting matter."

As a result of a vastly increased awareness of human psychic potential and an intensified interest in acupuncture, psionics, and radionics by the mass media, a number of new psychic research groups have sprung up throughout North and South America and Europe. Although there are a number of reputable organizations in the United States, two of the more reliable and sincere are the Institute of Noetic Sciences on the west coast and Mankind Research Unlimited, Inc., in Washington, D.C.

Headed by ex-astronaut Edgar Mitchell (*the sixth man on*

the Moon), its founder-president, the Institute of Noetic Sciences derives its name from the Greek root word *nous*—"Mind." Hence the study of Mind and Consciousness is called Noetics. The symbol adopted by the Institute was inspired by Teilhard de Chardin. The last letter of the Greek alphabet, omega (in three dimensions), points toward the constellation of Aquarius, indicating that through *Gnosis*—direct or intuitive knowledge surpassing the rational intellect—humanity can move toward an "Aquarian Age" of peace and fulfillment.

"This subjective knowing is a nonrational, cognitive process largely overlooked by the scientific world," Mitchell says. "Consciousness appears to be the central, unifying concept behind these different aspects of Mind."

The Institute of Noetic Sciences is located at 575 Middlefield Road, Palo Alto, California 94301, and has established five professorial research chairs, the first of which was named the Dr. Wernher von Braun Chair for the Study of Consciousness and the Physical Sciences. Dr. von Braun dedicated the chair in late February, 1975 in San Francisco.

Mankind Research Unlimited, Inc. appears to be most expert in the practical use of psionics and the development of a new line of radionics devices and psionics machines. Carl Schleicher, an Annapolis graduate and one-time ship-of-the-line Navy officer, is research and development director of Mankind Research, which is located at 1143 New Hampshire Avenue. N.W. Washington, D.C. 20037.

Schleicher engaged in advanced studies at the Universities of Cologne and Bonn, West Germany, at Lund, Sweden, and at American University. He is convinced that "We are now experiencing a kind of second Copernican era in science. The original era radically altered man's cherished conceptions about the Universe. Today's revolution, however, promises to revise man's concepts about his own nature and relationship to the Universe—seen and unseen—around him. The biological effects of our environment can be modified by the force field or energy symbolized by Mind—*either to enhance or threaten the well-being of man.*"

MRU has almost unlimited laboratory and research facilities in a dozen or more cities. Its specialties include acupuncture, psionics, biofeedback, EEG analysis, Mind and brain control, bioluminescence, psychophysics, bionics, biophysics, plasma physics, magnetohydrodynamics, cybernetics, cytology, psycho-acoustics, radionics (*therapy and diagnostic techniques*), biocybernetics, and psychotechnology research.

And that's just the beginning.

In his book, *The Soul of the Universe,** astrophysicist Dr. Gustaf Stromberg concluded that a purposeful organization of living structures and relationships exists between Mind and matter. "Human memory is probably indestructible and the *essence* of every living thing is immortal," he said. "This confirms the existence of a World Soul—or God."

But if memory and the essence of our being (the L-field and T-field) are immortal, what is death?

And what happens afterward?

*Gustaf Stromberg, *The Soul of the Universe*, Cambridge University Press, New York, 1940.

Chapter Ten

Beyond Death

A tall, sun-bronzed mountaineer carefully edged his way across a razor-sharp shelf of ice high in the Siegfried-Atlas glacier.

He stepped into the sun's dazzling glare and terror exploded in his mind as the ice groaned and gave way underfoot. Half sliding and half falling down the precipice, he felt his restraining rope catch him, hold for a brief instant, then saw back and forth across the keen-edged ice and shred apart.

His companions watched with helpless horror as he plummeted at a crazy angle across the glacier's searing white face. Halfway to the bottom, his body was flipped upside down by a violent gale and slammed backward into an ice promonotory a hundred feet below.

It took the better part of an hour for his rescuers to negotiate the arduous descent. All this time his body lay in a twisted, motionless heap, his life's blood saturating the hard-packed snow.

Miraculously, he survived to add his testimony to that of hundreds of others who had come close to a violent death. His description was almost a perfect echo of their own experiences: "My whole life flashed by . . . everything was transfigured as though by a heavenly light and everything was beautiful—without grief, anxiety or pain. I felt no conflict or strife. A divine calm swept my soul, blending the objective observations with subjective feelings. Then I heard a thud and my fall was over."

What, exactly, is death? Is it total obliteration—or, do you survive?

Almost traditionally, death has been considered an indeli-

157

cate if not morbid subject. But now an emerging "science of consciousness" is beginning to change this attitude. One result is that, contrary to popular belief and fear, death is not something to be dreaded. "Socially and culturally, we seem on our way to becoming a new species," said Dr. Lewis Thomas in the medical journal *Pharos*. "Before long we will talk as openly about death as we do now about sex, or money."

All the evidence gathered by psionics and L-field researchers indicates that consciousness—"the real you"—is eternal.

But until recently, subjective death experiences were ignored by science. Even parapsychology—usually more interested in the ESP experiences of *relatives* of the dying or dead person—looked askance at them. Then Dr. Karlis Osis, the slender Latvian director of the American Society for Psychical Research, published his unique pilot study titled "Deathbed Observations by Physicians and Nurses." In it, he distilled and analyzed 1370 eyewitness reports from 10,000 nurses and doctors who had had close communication with dying patients.

A characteristic pattern emerged: dying people often experienced a kind of transcendent "reality" that they could not express in words. At death, a kind of superconsciousness seems to be "switched over" to the immortal L-field.

After years of computer-processing his data, Dr. Osis spent another two years duplicating his original study—this time however from a group of hospitals in India. The results were the same in the land of the Buddha and Hinduism as it was in Western, Judeo-Christian cultures: at the edge of death, dying people tend to see visions and often become ecstatically happy. This "switchover" or transfer of consciousness, it seems, cannot occur without the cooperation of the higher-energy field—the L-field.

Dr. Lewis Thomas, former dean of the Yale University School of Medicine however, sees death from a purely physical viewpoint. "Dying involves the adjournment of enormous numbers of cells," he says, "and the end of all collaborative action between them. The central administrative mechanisms are turned off; the heart stops, the brain stops, and that's the end of life for the organism . . . it is decentralization that initiates the death of the whole organism."

The mechanistic description doesn't and cannot account for the inexplicable ecstasy of many dying people. Yet some of the Indian physicians and nurses in Dr. Osis' current study are as skeptical about the euphoria of terminal patients as their American and European counterparts. They too attributed the visions and ecstasy of dying people to cerebral anoxia—an insufficient supply of blood (and oxygen) to the brain.

Similar to the slow, often peaceful death of hospital patients, some near-victims of violent death also experience euphoria and have transcendental experiences or sensations. But these can't be attributed to cerebral anoxia. Surprisingly enough, whether the death is peaceful or violent there's no proof that death is a painful experience, much less an agonizing one. Nature, apparently, is deliberately benevolent—even merciful.

This was dramatically underscored by an adventure of the famous British explorer, David Livingstone. While he was on expedition in East Africa, a charging lion nearly tore him apart. The big cat, which had been wounded, sprang from the bush and closed its jaws across the explorer's right chest and shoulder; its teeth sank into his throat, fractured his upper humerus and crushed his thorax before his gun bearers managed to kill the animal.

Livingstone survived and recovered, but he was so puzzled by the fact that he'd felt no pain that he wrote a complete description of the episode. "Surprisingly, I felt no fear or alarm. In fact I had the most extraordinary sense of calm and detachment," he reminisced. "It was so peaceful as to be almost pleasurable."

He concluded that Nature provides every living thing with *a protective mechanism* that is somehow "switched on at the time of impending death and carries the organism through the experience in a haze of tranquility." Such testimony confirms the observation that the withdrawal of the L-field from the body is accompanied by subjective, inexpressible joy.

A psychiatrist from the University of Iowa, Dr. Russell Noyes, investigated near-fatal encounters with sudden death by healthy, clear-minded people and discovered a three-segmented pattern: 1) when the victim realizes that his struggles are futile, he calmly accepts the inevitable; 2) a flash "review" of his past life takes place; 3) this is followed by an intense feeling of transcendental joy. In many cases, the dying person seems to encounter an environment and/or state of being that seems "familiar."

Among people who have had automobile accidents, falls, or other close calls with death, Dr. Noyes observed that "when even a slight possibility of survival remains, alertness to the danger is increased along with the physical and mental energy to meet it. But if the danger is not overcome, the victim surrenders to a feeling of passive resignation, which in turn leads to a sensation of profound tranquility."

This was the experience of Albert Heim, a Swiss professor of geology when he slipped and fell from a cliff in the Santis Mountain Range. He "knew" instantly that the fall would kill him. A sense of profound calm and timelessness followed. His past life flashed by in a series of extremely vivid pictures. "It was as though I looked out the window of a high house," he said. "I saw myself as a seven-year-old boy going to school, I then saw myself in the fourth-grade classroom with a beloved teacher. I saw my life as though I were an actor on stage upon which I looked down from the highest gallery in the theater ... I wasn't in the least concerned about invoking God's help. I had the feeling of submission to necessity."

There was no fear, grief, or pain. Some part of his psyche "watched" the fall with a kind of amused detachment. He *heard* his impact, but there was no agony, no pain. The "system" was prepared for the L-field's withdrawal.

"Death is not a dreadful experience," Dr. Thomas reiterated. "Certain mechanisms seem designed to guide and care for every organism through the stages of dying. Once a prescribed point in the process is reached, fear is replaced by tranquility and acceptance—often joy." Similar reports from other parts of the world statistically point up the possibility that the Self or individual personality may actually continue existing in a timeless condition of supreme joy and rapture.

An outstanding incident from Dr. Noyes' study involved a highly intelligent trained nurse who nearly died of anaphylactic shock from a penicillin allergy. She was so moved by "the state of joyous enchantment when the curtains were parted" that she swore she would never fear dying again.

As soon as she swallowed the tablet it occurred to her that she might be allergic. Then, as her breathing became difficult and she realized that she was actually dying, she was filled with terror and put up a brief, desperate struggle to live. But the "mechanism" of the dying process was suddenly "switched on" and her fear instantly vanished. In its place came the calm realization that death was not only inevitable but actually *desirable.*

"When she accepted the idea of her death," Dr. Noyes said, "the second, or life review phase, began. This was followed by the third stage consisting of mystical phenomena . . . in rapid fire she 'watched' a great many scenes from her life." Intensely brilliant colors impressed her—first, a beloved doll from her childhood with brilliantly blue glass eyes. Then she saw herself riding a bright red bicycle on an equally bright green lawn. These fleeting glimpses of her life "made me ecstatically happy," she said afterward.* Her life review was followed by a profound sense of "belonging"—a condition she reported as "indescribable bliss" and "ecstasy."

While such reports are of subjective experiences with death, they seem to possess an integrity of their own. It's difficult, however, for most scientists to accept the evidence without some kind of repeatable experimentation, and since no such experiment is conceivable, the case for postmortem survival seems to be inherently unprovable—scientifically, at any rate.

Predictably, Dr. Osis believes that a definite pattern is emerging from his work. Under different conditions, at different times and places, people from diverse backgrounds report essentially the same kind of death experience.

A gifted poet named Caresse Crosby gave these impressions of her own death by drowning.* When my head plunged beneath the water, I took one long frightened gulp and I never got another breath of air. My lungs expelled once and refilled with tide water. The blood rushed from my toes to my nose and suddenly my head seemed to expand and ex-

---

*Caresse Crosby, *The Passionate Years,* Dial Press, New York, 1953.

plode, but softly as though it were a cotton ball fluffing out and out and out. Into my ears the waters poured strange lullabies and little by little, there beneath the flood a dazzling prismatic effulgence cleared my vision—not only did I see and hear harmony, but I understood everything. And slowly, as a bubble rises to the surface, I rose to the surface, rose up through the wooden platform, rose to where I could dominate the whole scene spread out beneath me. I watched my father at work on his boat, my brothers deathly frightened hanging to my spindly heels and I, my hair like seaweed pulled flat against the submerged bottom of the float. Thus, while I drowned I saw my father turn and act; I saw my frightened brothers run homewards; I saw the efforts to bring me back to life and *I tried not to come back.*

"It was the most perfect state of easeful joy that I ever experienced, then or since. There was no sadness or sickness from which I wished to escape ... that moment in all my life has never been equalled for pure happiness. Could I have glimpsed, while drowned (for I *was* drowned) the freedom of eternal life? One thing I know, that Nirvana does exist between here and the hereafter—a space of delight, for I have been there."

Is this actually what happens? We can't imagine our own death, so our minds simply reject the idea. "The fact that one's own death is inconceivable," said one dedicated family doctor, "indicates the possibility of survival. Personally, I would like to believe that we don't go to oblivion, but that we survive and are reincarnated."

Be that as it may, the subject of death is "coming out of the closet." When a college student was asked his definition of death, he replied, "I feel it's the end of something, and sometimes the beginning of something else. I can't believe you just stop living all of a sudden. I don't know. I think there's got to be something after it."

This seems to reflect most people's feelings. During a poll taken by the American Institute of Public Opinion, 74 percent of the American public said they definitely believed in life after death; 14 percent said they didn't, and 12 percent were undecided.

Three quarters of the terminal patients in the deathbed observations gathered by Dr. Karlis Osis hallucinated apparitions of deceased friends or relatives. Those who were heavily sedated, drugged, or only partially conscious tended to hallucinate living people, demons, or religious figures. Undrugged, conscious, and rational patients, however, saw apparitions of deceased friends and relatives—*in some cases even when the patient was completely unaware that these people had died!*

"The odds," says Dr. Osis, "are astronomical against such a broad discrepancy. It would appear that most of the hallucinations of the dead are not a function of being unconscious or delirious, but has deeper roots."

The evidence seems to support his theory. In *Deathbed Visions,* * Sir William Barrett told of the impending death of a woman in a London hospital. Because of her own terminal illness, the news that her sister Vida had died three weeks previously had been kept from her. As her own death grew closer, the patient initially complained, "It's so dark—so dark I can't see . . ." A few seconds later however, she said cheerfully, "Oh, it's so lovely and bright; you cannot see as I can." Then she seemed puzzled by something. "I can see father; he wants me to come with him." Her expression suddenly changed to astonishment. "He has Vida with him!" She smiled and gripped her mother's hand. "Vida is with him!"

Moments later she died, the smile still on her face.

The fact that some dying patients seem to see dead persons is called the "Peak in Darien" experience by psychic researchers. The idea is that the spirits of dead relatives come to help the dying person and to "take them away to another world." So far there's nothing to explain why a dying patient should see a deceased person about whose death he or she knows nothing.

Author Wainwright Evans described the death of a close friend in *Tomorrow* magazine: "In his last hours, John Thompson was sitting up in bed, propped by a pillow because of a heart condition. He knew he was going to die; his mind was clear; and he had a look, not so much of resignation as of complete and happy acceptance."

As the patient looked toward the foot of the bed, his face

*Sir William Barrett, *Deathbed Visions,* Methuen, London, c. 1926.

beamed with happiness. "Why, there's Emmy," he exclaimed. "There's Bill!" (Emmy and Bill were long-deceased friends of his youth. She had been bridesmaid and he the best man at his wedding.) A few hours later he died, "witha joyful smile on his face that seemed to speak of the peace in his heart."

In his autobiography, Carl Gustav Jung tells how, after a severe heart attack, he "hung on to the edge of death." He separated from his body and found himself floating away from the Earth, which he saw from a thousand miles overhead (exactly as we now know it appears from space) "bathed in a glorious blue and white light." He told of feelings of universal unity, ineffability, a transcendence of time and space, a sense of truth, loss of control, intense emotion, and intense joy.

He then approached a temple, "the door of which was surrounded by a wreath of flames," Jung wrote. "I had the feeling that everything was being sloughed away; everything I aimed at or wished for or thought, the whole phantasmagoria of earthly existence fell away or was stripped from me ... I had the certainty that I was about to enter an illuminated room and would meet there all those people to whom I belong in reality. There I would at last understand—this too was a certainty—what historical nexus I or my life fitted into."

Next he found himself in the most serene and lovely environment he could have imagined—a kind of enchanted garden through which he passed en route to an even greater experience: "It is impossible to convey the beauty and intensity of emotion during these visions. They were the most tremendous things I have ever experienced ... I can only describe it as the ecstasy of a nontemporal state, in which present, past and future are one. Everything that happens in time had been brought together into a concrete whole, yet I observed it with complete objectivity."

In cases where children who have survived death refer to feelings of indescribable beauty and happiness, it seems to strengthen the case for the profound tranquility of death—if not survival. Twenty-five percent of these experiences studied by Dr. Noyes came closest to the final stage of life. Here, the dying person feels that he has gone "beyond the boundaries of past and future." This level is characterized by flashes of light, ecstasy, visions, and the presence of what one subject described as "an incredibly benign outside force." Survivors tell much the same story—whether death is threatened by a fall, asphyxiation, a heart attack, or drowning.

There are occasional variations of the "Peak in Darien" experience. Before his death by cancer in November 1973, actor Lawrence Harvey, according to his widow, Paulene Stone, achieved profound inner peace and was helped to overcome the fear of death by Dr. William Lang, a renowned London eye surgeon—*who had died in 1937!*

When he learned that he was riddled with cancer, the 45-year-old Harvey consulted a psychic healer named George Chapman, who claimed that he is guided by the spirit of Dr. Lang. Although Harvey was greatly relieved of his pain, Chapman said, "When I came out of the trance that first time, Larry told me the doctor had broken the news that he could not be saved and would die before Christmas."

Mrs. Harvey revealed a surprising, possibly unique development: "Larry liked Mr. Chapman immensely," she said, "much better than he liked Dr. Lang, who was very abrupt and much drier with him."

Stories of psychic healing and out-of-body experiences are receiving widespread and uncritical acceptance. Orthodox psychologists, however, generally think that the alleged separation of the Self from the physical body—as Jung described it—is simply the negation of death by the subconscious. ("The victim may see his body as near death but by placing himself outside of it he is able to witness the scene with detachment.")

Freud, the father of psychoanalysis, who also was intrigued by the human tendency to ignore or eliminate death: "Whenever we make the attempt to imagine our own death we can perceive that we really survive as spectators. Hence no one believes in his own death . . . in our unconscious minds every one of us is convinced of his own immortality."

If this is the psychology of death, why the feelings of ecstasy, transcendence, and life review? In close escapes from violent death, the panorama of the past is often relived in a vivid, lightning-like flash. According to Dr. Noyes, "This fleeting return to past memories may result from the sudden loss of future time orientation. Memories of people now dead, so intensely vivid that they seem real, are characteristically reported during the acute stages of grief. They may symbolize a clinging to or search for a lost loved one."

Here again the orthodox explanation is that dying people hang on to the only thing that connects them with life—their memories of physical existence, which become more precious and sharply focused at the moment they are about to be lost. In the final review of life the dying man often experiences an incredibly passionate belief in the indescribable meaning of all existence. He somehow manages to fit this into what he perceives as the order of the Universe. And as one skeptic stated, "The dread book of account of which the scriptures speak is contained in the mind of each individual." In other words, we pass judgement on ourselves at the moment of death.

The most dramatic death experience of all is transcendence—the final stage. The dying person then seems to experience his essential being in a uniquely different way. The sheer intensity of emotion at this stage is only equalled by the inability of words to express it. Jung described it as "a nontemporal state in which I was beyond time, beyond the past and future—in eternity."

The great astronomer Johannes Kepler, as much a mystic as he was a mathematician, was keenly interested in death and survival: "The human soul is a part of Nature; its essence cannot be divided from it ... all souls have a continuous relation to the one world-soul or the Metathron, as has the sunlight to the sun. Consequently, multiplicity really lies in matter and not in form, which is nothing but a continuous emanation from God, or the Word of God, imparting life and being to all creatures. When it is withdrawn, life is revoked."

Kepler's outlook is echoed by Dr. Irving Cohen, a sympathetic family doctor from Commack, Long Island. "I firmly believe in, well—let's call it a Life Source," he said. "My philosophy is that this Life Source cannot die and that we're all connected to and dependent on it to replenish our cells and generate the power to keep our bodies functioning. When we die, it's as if the cord is disconnected and the body stops. So does the brain, but not the Mind. In some mysterious way the personality and total life experience continues—as though it rejoins this Life Source. The way our minds work is too wonderful, too magnificent, too marvelous to be the product of chance or blind evolution.

"Unless we're deaf, dumb and blind, we simply have to perceive a higher power or intelligence. Look at the way our bodies are put together; look at its chemistry and the way it functions. The whole mechanism is brilliant beyond human comprehension. The intelligence, or pattern, simply *can't* be obliterated by physical death."

Is this what the transcendent stage of dying implies? Psychologist William James calls this achievement of inner illumination its "noetic quality," a condition typified by a sense of overpowering but inexpressible truth. Once the dying person has grasped the harmonious structure of the universal order, he seems profoundly convinced that life on a much higher and more exciting level transcends the death of the physical body.

Both William James and Carl Jung believed that such feelings are real and that they demanded scientific study. They were convinced that our normal waking awareness is just a small part of the total human consciousness. A century ago the British Society for Psychical Research suggested that reports of these experiences "must be sifted and tested, and run the gauntlet of confrontation with the total context of experience just like what comes from the outer world of sense. Since we are not mystics ourselves, their value must be checked by empirical methods."

This is what Dr. Osis, Dr. Noyes, and others are now doing. As a result, the rapid advance of thanatology (the scientific study of death, its causes and phenomena) raises questions that seem to indicate that life may be more than a biological accident or some mindless reaction of evolution.

In "The Death of Ivan Ilyich," Leo Tolstoy tells of a dying man's transcendence: " . . . all he had been tortured by was now falling away of itself, falling on two sides, ten sides, all sides at once. He searched for his accustomed fear of death and could not find it. Where was death? What was death?

There was no fear because there was no death. There was light instead of death."

At the very least the evidence indicates that death need not be an agonizing or terrifying experience. At best, it may be the ultimate transcending, fulfilling experience—one that gives life meaning, even joy. The case for continued existence, at least as far as physical science is concerned, seems to be inherently unprovable. But even if the accumulated evidence doesn't warrant such faith, it makes life infinitely more meaningful and equips every one of us to meet death with courage, dignity—and hope.

Chapter Eleven

Contact!

Next to coming face to face with Almighty God, man's first contact with a species of intelligent, nonhuman being is destined to be the most electrifying, mind-shattering, and stupendous event in history. It will transcend the impact of all previous human experience and it will probably happen by 1982.

mic influence is a necessary prerequisite to interspecies confrontation. Science is evolving toward understanding of the "nonphysical"—that is, newer and more sophisticated

A totally different understanding of energy fields and cos-concepts of Life, Consciousness, and Intelligence.

No matter how distant or strange nonhuman intelligence may eventually appear, specialists who study the electrodynamic Fields of Life believe that all life throughout the Universe *must* share certain common characteristics.

One of these is the interpenetration of a kind of "electromagnetic matrix" with all physical bodies. Soviet experiments with Kirlian photography have shown that these L-fields (the Fields of Life) surround every living thing like a pulsating, multicolored aura and interact with the total Life Energy of the Universe.

The Earth's magnetic field is flattened, pulled, pushed, and otherwise influenced by the solar wind, by the Sun's powerful magnetic field, as well as that of the Moon and planets. These forces affect terrestrial weather, the ion count in the atmosphere, and man's own biomagnetic and psychic reaction to them.

This is a simplified summary of how cosmic influences work. It also suggests that the astrology of our solar system is a purely local phenomenon. However, the same conditions

169

must also be true for every star and planetary system in the Galaxy. The "biologic" energy fields involved in these cosmic influences seem to be a good basis for interspecies contact.

The mysterious "instructions" for the growth of cells, the healing of wounds and broken bones comes from the overriding matrix or L-field. The more complex L-fields, such as those found in human beings, can be modified by the application of artificial magnetism. But the more refined T-fields are of paramount importance.

These human thought fields are similar to gravity inasmuch as they act at a distance and through barriers. Even Faraday cages that block out all or most of the electromagnetic spectrum present no obstacle to telepathic transmission.

Sooner or later, advanced alien civilizations that may have scientifically discovered astrology and mastered the influence of their own local cosmic environment should eventually uncover the secrets of these indestructable electrical matrixes—the L-fields and T-fields. Once a species learns this, the stage is set for direct, instantaneous communication with other intelligent beings.

The following story indicates that this earthshaking event may already have taken place in California. (If so, the great radio-telescope search for intelligent signals from space civilizations could already be obsolete. The superfine emanations of high-power energy fields seem to be entirely different from the electromagnetic spectrum because they are detected by instruments that bar all electrical and magnetic energy.)

The Ecola Institute of California, which specializes in environmental and conceptive space research for NASA, reported receiving such signals late in 1971. The pulses were recorded with instruments which no existing radio telescope can duplicate. They are, according to Ecola's managing director, L. George Lawrence, from *beyond* the electromagnetic spectrum!

This new kind of energy is somehow related to gravity and is postulated as the vehicle for the transmissions. Physical science can no more fathom this mystery than it can explain gravity, electricity, or other forms of energy such as telepathy. The evidence suggests that instantaneous communication is now going on among the stars of our Galaxy—and beyond—with about the same ease with which we place a telephone call to Europe.

This startling discovery in the Mojave Desert has yet to be fully confirmed by independent researchers, but scientific journals and papers have published several reports about the technological details of Lawrence's discovery. On October 29, 1971, he was conducting a field test to prove that plant life generates biological signals. With extremely sophisticated instruments, he picked up these emanations from local flora at a distance. For about 30 minutes prior to this, his instrument package had been accidentally pointed at the constellation Ursa Major. During this period it received signals Lawrence immediately recognized as being "biological" in origin. Except that they originated from outer space, they were very much like the signals his instruments picked up from the plant life in the Mojave Desert.

They were repetitive, indicating a nonrandom origin. And since his instruments were shielded by a Faraday tube, they apparently could *not* have been transmitted by way of the known electromagnetic spectrum. Moreover, their point of origin was far beyond the reach of any transmissions capable of being generated by human power.

By converting direct current to alternating current, he translated the signals from space into audible sounds which he recorded on tape. The repetitive warbling, woof-like sounds caused a chill of excitement to race up and down his spine. Listening intently, Lawrence slipped the headphones partially off and sat bolt upright on his cot. Through the gathering dusk his eyes traced the silhouette of the six-inch refractor telescope jutting out among the complex array of electronics and optical instruments.

The Faraday tube was mounted on the telescope. Lawrence took a "fix" and snapped on the recorder. When he increased the volume, the warbling took on an exotic character which he found to be definitely pleasurable.

During a small eternity the enraptured engineer seemed to be almost transported to that other world. It took a sheer effort of will to shake off the feeling and force his mind back to a more objective analysis of what was happening. He smothered his excitement and fed a local pilot tone onto the tape. This is a steady signal used as background sound against which to check tape speed and other variables.

During this time Lawrence was acutely conscious of being alone. He studied the angle of the telescope, drew an imaginary "bead" to the nearest stars at which it was pointed, and double-checked it on the faintly illuminated panel of a synchronous star map.

The nonelectromagnetic signal was coming strongly and steadily from the direction of Ursa Major. No other equipment could have detected it. Lawrence shook his head and gazed across the almost featureless lava bed in the gathering chill of the October night. He felt strangely reassured by these electronic extensions of his limited physical senses.

The delicate instruments faithfully recorded the strange signals from some perhaps-unimaginable species of intelligent beings—a species that could have been ancient before the Earth itself was born! His head swam. They might even have originated from a genus that had learned millions of years ago to communicate on this "biological" band—the kind that Dr. Harold S. Burr, Hunt Professor of Anatomy (Emeritus) of the Yale School of Medicine, recently characterized as the Universal, all-pervading "L-field."

It was conceivable therefore, that *electromagnetic*-based communication among advanced civilizations in the Galaxy was obsolete.

Why worry about the speed of light "barrier" when instantaneous communication between star systems may be possible? An "L-field," the invisible matrix around which living matter forms, could permit transmission of data at velocities far exceeding light speed. Lawrence reminded himself that he was a scientist of no mean achievement—an expert oceanographer, historian, cartographer, originator of the world's first laser engine, and the author of 46 books and articles.

As the managing director of the Ecola Institute (*currently engaged in nuclear radiation research, medical and agricultural biomagnetic research, and conceptive space research for NASA among other studies*), L. George Lawrence had his work cut out for him. He was awestruck by the monumental significance of this discovery.

The first widespread data on these L-fields was published in 1966 when polygraph expert Cleve Backster detected the psychogalvanic reaction of an office plant that was rigged up to a lie detector while it was being watered. Backster wanted to learn how long the moisture took to reach the leaves, but he was astonished when the plant gave a reading exactly like that of a human being under strong emotional stimulation. On impulse, he decided to burn one leaf of the plant, but— *before* he could light a match—*in fact as soon as the thought occurred to him*—the polygraph recording needle fluctuated! Backster claims to have gotten the same reactions in a series of rigidly controlled scientific tests involving myriad other life forms, both plant and animal.

The stems and leaves of other flowers and plants, even when cut or shredded into pieces, he reported, reacted to *thoughts* of violence just as the original plant had. Two philodendrons placed in distant rooms also responded with what might have been the plant equivalent of "horror" to the violent deaths of brine shrimp which were exterminated by dumping them into boiling water. This was tantamount to ESP in humans. Even at a distance, through a series of closed doors and under strictly controlled conditions, the plants reacted to the violent death of *other* life forms. Backster's experiments were published in detail in the Winter, 1968, issue of the *International Journal of Parapsychology*. It was the first scientific evidence—in reverse—of the "old wives' tale" about plants responding to human love and affection.

In the growth and development of science during the past few centuries, each new advance compounded the natural evolvement of new "discovery" built on existing knowledge, whether or not that knowledge was generally known and accepted by orthodoxy. Every great electrical genius, (including Einstein, Tesla, Marconi, Steinmetz, and Edison) with direct personal experience in biomagnetics has reached the conclusion that the human mind is the key that will eventually unlock the mysteries of the Universe. Not, however, by the standard academic route.

We cannot conceive of phenomena that, in the literal sense, are *impossible*. Anything that violates the underlying laws of the Universe—whether we are aware of these laws or not—*cannot exist*. In other words, anything that *does* exist is, *ipso facto* an integral part of the Universe and must therefore have a place, and *purpose*. Nature does *not* create entities or endow them with definite characteristics—without a *specific* reason.

Consciousness, awareness, and intelligence, therefore, are properties of the intangible but all-important force that, for lack of a better term, we call MIND. Mind *exists*, therefore it must serve some purpose in this Universe. As Dr. Wayne Batteau of M.I.T. once put it, "The Universe is crammed with information. Man's job is to read it out."

But there is too great a concentration on tradition and authority, thus tightening the web of scientific bureaucracy instead of staying close to truth through hard, basic research. In a way, science is like religion was during the Middle Ages—ultraconservative, traditionalist, organization-conscious, and quick to condemn any notion (usually without study) that lies outside its own rigidly defined rules. Nature is no respecter of man's laws.

The great mathematician and philosopher, Albert Einstein, once remarked: "God does *not* play dice with the Universe."

Characteristically, the Universe we know is *teleological* in that everything operates within predictable laws. Man does not know *all* these laws, in fact the combined mental energy of the entire human race, from "Creation" to whatever "end" there may be—*and be it known that this includes the greatest scientific minds in history*—couldn't even *begin* to learn, say, one ten thousand billionth of one percent of what there is to know.

From time to time, when men like Marconi, Tesla, and Edison reported unexplained signals from space (on a non-electromagnetic "beam"), some were effectively prevented from further research by the simple expedient of withdrawing money from their projects. As a result, Tesla nurtured a certain bitterness toward General Electric and Steinmetz's relations with Westinghouse were strained. Despite their claims to the contrary, Big Science and Big Business have no interest in what they call "nonproductive, dead-end research."

Yet in spite of the ridicule of the materialists, the idea that there are other worlds—even other star systems—like our own has gradually become an integral part of our Mass Consciousness. Only three decades ago, no "respectable" course in astronomy or physics would acknowledge the *idea* that intelligent beings might exist somewhere other than Earth.

The Holy Office of the Inquisition of the medieval Church also persecuted anyone who proclaimed that the Earth was *not* "the center of the Universe." Giordano Bruno, formerly a Dominican priest, was actually burned at the stake in 1600 simply for teaching what everyone knows today: that billions of blazing suns are responsible for the whiteness of the Milky Way. "It is composed," he said, "of numberless other worlds, some of them even more glorious than our own . . ."

To hidebound traditionalists, this is *still* heresy. Because, they claim, "Nobody has ever proven that any other star has planets like the Sun. We may be unique in the Universe, but we'll never know one way or the other because interstellar space voyages are now and will be forever impossible." Believe it or not, these are the exact words of Dr. Forrest Ray Moulton, the foremost astronomer in America between the 1930s and 1940s. Every age has had its Moultons.

Because of the vastness of "empty" space between the stars, a large number of astronomers are extremely pessimistic about getting to the stars. "Even if it *were* possible to build a ship capable of reaching the stars, it would take a whole generation just to reach the nearest one—and *another* generation to return. Who's going to underwrite an experiment that long?"

Perhaps no one will have to. The way it looks now, trillions of billions of civilized beings throughout the galaxy may be within *easy* hailing distance. If intelligent, alien beings *are* trying to get through to us, it may be that our radio telescopes are sensitive *only* to the limited electromagnetic spectrum.

Speculation? Certainly, but according to Sir James Jeans, "Today there is a wide measure of agreement . . . that the stream of knowledge is heading toward a non-mechanical reality; the Universe begins to look more like a great *thought* than a great machine. Mind no longer appears as an accidental intruder into the realm of matter; we are beginning to suspect that we ought rather to hail it as the creator and governor of the realm of matter ... The Universe may not only be queerer than we think, it may be queerer than we're *able* to think!"

Even in the known electromagnetic spectrum—without considering the (to us) "astounding" possibility of a "short cut" which would enable an energy field to attain a "velocity" (the best term conceivable) of many times the speed of light, it's a miracle that these fields can be "frozen" into what we regard as solid matter. Yet this "marriage" of the physical with the realm of the Mind is congruent with presently known scientific fact.

Still, a breakthrough of unprecedented dimensions is imminent in our understanding of gravity, electricity, human thought, and new concepts of matter and energy. This will pave the way for the next step in the great adventure of our species—the construction of revolutionary new engines—space drives of a completely radical design that will enable us to reach the distant stars, other worlds, and other civilizations—*within our lifespans!*

The Soviet Academy of Sciences is known to be hot on the trail of breaking the secret "code" of the cohesive force we call gravity and to find a practical method of harnessing the new power to drive the mighty engines of tomorrow.

The great thinkers and writers of past history were forced to convey their knowledge in similes, parables, and symbols and (even so) with great indirection and restraint. They recognized that Nature's invisible "barrier" presented an impassible obstacle to the understanding of their ideas *during their lifetimes.* An examination of some of the great classics reveals that many of these scientists, philosophers, and mathematicians camouflaged their messages. This "code" was unrecognizable except to a few of their enlightened contemporaries. This is how the priests and "magicians" of ancient days disguised arcane or forbidden knowledge from the "profane" masses.

Much of what is regarded today as wizardry, alchemy, witchcraft, astrology, and other forms of "sorcery"—the secret rites into which only select apprentices were initiated—are in fact some of today's commonly accepted scientific facts. If Galileo, for example, had tried to weigh a bladder of air or construct a "magical instrument" of glass lenses to magnify the planets even a *century* before his time, he would have suffered the same fate as Giordano Bruno.

Writers like Lewis Carroll, author of *Alice's Adventures in Wonderland,* and Dean Jonathan Swift, who wrote *Gulliver's Travels,* knew mathematics, medicine, and astronomy and were well in advance of their time, but they were forced to write satire, which was believed to be written solely for children. This could be true of other flights of fantasy such as *The Arabian Nights,* tales about the voyages of Sinbad, and the entire gamut of "fabulous" old writings.

In 1513 a Turkish admiral named Piri Reis obtained what was probably the greatest collection of copies of copies (of copies) of world maps based on ancient Roman, Phoenician, Greek, Babylonian, and Sumerian cartographers. Only a fragment of the Piri Reis map has survived, but it is obviously an aerial map of the world whose original plate or plates were made in 4000 B.C., perhaps earlier.

According to the opinions of modern cartographic experts, a data system was focused on various points and finally zeroed in on the site of what is now Cairo, Egypt, and took the picture of the globe in one shot. The Piri Reis map looked bizarre and out of shape because of foreshortening and geometric distortions. Since the Turkish admiral's time, other cartographers were unable to make any sense of it until some staff members of the U.S. Hydrographic Office in Washington, D.C. developed a modern grid which enabled them to make a conventional projection. At this point, an exciting discovery was made. Not only did the map exhibit now surface features of the Earth, but the outline of completely unknown land masses in the Antarctic!

Then, during the International Geophysical Year beginning in 1957, U.S. Task Force 143 made seismic soundings through ice sheets that were 10,000 feet deep. The ancient Piri Reis map was vindicated as an absolutely accurate document in every detail, authentically made (in its original form) from a point far out in space—*over four millennia ago!*

Who or what made the original cartographic record from

space? And, to quote the title of Nobel laureate Enrico Fermi's book, *"Where Are They?"*

The recent experiences of L. George Lawrence, especially his "biological" recording (the original of which is now held in the scientific archives of the Smithsonian Institution in Washington, D.C.) is probably the most tangible evidence yet of extraterrestrial intelligence.

He is the author of articles in foreign and American magazines such as *Electronics World,* the *Electrical Review, Popular Electronics,* and other scientific technical and popular publications. Lawrence made his momentous discovery *after* writing an article called "Interstellar Communications" which appeared in the October 1971 issue of *Electronics World.* He wrote, " . . . we actually made an effort to discern the great Indian legend of a lost starship, said to be buried deep beneath the floor of the Mojave Desert near Pisgah Crater (near Interstate 40). According to the heavily embroidered Indian legend, an enormous starship triggered massive lava flows in the sensitive geology after landing and sinking into great depths.

"We used an electronic magnetometer during our brief geophysical survey, trying to determine pulsating or residual electromagnetic radiation implied to be radiated by the starship's standby engine, if any."

The evidence Lawrence presents for this gratuitous assumption is the photograph of a field magnetometer in front of the Pisgah lava beds covering part of Lavic Dry Lake. He is seen gazing at the profile of the Mountain of the Bearded God about eight miles in the distance.

Lawrence explained why this geological survey was a failure. "When hot lava cools down in the geomagnetic field of the Earth, it acquires what is technically known as 'thermoremanent' magnetization. The molecules in the lava assume a magnetic state which confuses an instrument such as a magnetometer. It could indicate sub-basement fields where none exist."

Lawrence, however, is undaunted by the failure. "We believe that exploratory aids such as geophysical gravimeters and applied seismometry would be superior to magnetometry, because depth-ranging provides better diagnostic data. Unfortunately, the enormous lava overburden makes exploratory work extremely costly (millions of dollars would be involved and a large staff of scientific personnel) in order to reach into these depths. Many old Indians, including the late ancestor of one of the Chiefs who had related the legend passed on from generation to generation and finally to us, would never go near the lava beds."

He admits that it was pure enchantment with the old legend "plus the overpowering atmosphere one feels when looking at the Pisgah/Amboy volcanic systems," that prompted him to set up the second biodynamic field station in this region. "Plant population is sparse out here, quite precocious, but the ecology in general unspoiled."

Lawrence *presumes* the interstellar signals he received may have been "emergency transmissions." How could he *possibly* know a thing like that? On the other hand, how can we be so sure he *doesn't* know it?

"We ran some unsuccessful experiments in March and April," he said. "Then on April 10, 1972, at 22:30 Pacific Daylight Time, another apparent interstellar signal anomaly was noted. The phenomenon was weak, but lacked electromagnetic interferences."

He reports hearing other signals directly, but nothing as strong, steady, or emphatic as the transmission of October 1971. Moreover, he doesn't have the facilities for 24-hour astronomical surveillance, even though his equipment is being "upgraded." He believes these are truly interstellar emergency transmissions.

In some mysterious way, the Ecola Institute (Post Office Box 3284, San Bernardino, California 92413) monitors common electromagnetic interference from domestic, industrial, and/or stellar sources "in order to filter out non-living emanations in order to determine which are biological-type waves."

Carrying the theory that the signals may be "emergency transmissions" even further, Lawrence says, "Should these signals be of an emergency nature, it is unfortunate that no direct or indirect help could be offered. Perhaps a computer analysis of the October, '71 tape will provide clues. The sequences in the tape are, as you might notice, much too fast to permit a manual extraction of apparent data."

Yet he doesn't hold forth much hope for any available computer analysis of the tapes. "If these signals are indeed of a highly personal nature, no conceivable amount of 'modern computer technology can be applied to their evaluation. We simply do not yet have bionic-type computers which can collect seemingly random data and produce a concise readout. The U.S. Air Force, IBM and other computer people are working with such designs, but definite success may not be achieved within the next five years or so. The best computer is, of course, an organic type equipped with biological transducers—such as the *human brain*. So far, all efforts to duplicate this Nature-made instrument by means of electronic hardware have failed."

Attempts to create a "thinking, conscious" machine are still underway at MIT's Artificial Intelligence Group under "Project Mac," which is underwritten by funds from the Office of Naval Intelligence.

These attempts could result in failure unless the Essence of the Mind or T-field (which, as we have seen, can attach itself to the cerebral cortex, and presumably to other kinds of matter) is combined somehow with electronic circuitry.

That, however, could quite *literally* blow someone's mind!

When Dr. Wilder Penfield was director of the Montreal Neurological Institute, he performed brain operations on patients that were only under a light local anaesthetic. With tiny electrical currents applied to stimulate certain areas of the exposed cortex, Dr. Penfield could induce a patient to reexperience any part of his past—to subjectively relive any segment of his life—at will. To the patient, it seemed almost as "real" as if it was actually happening. Conversely, many biochemists are trying to prove that human memory is nothing but chemistry. So far, they have failed.

From his experiments, Dr. Penfield deduced that L-fields—Nature's "blueprints"—can be modified and are often overridden by the human thought field! Carried to its logical extension, this means that "intangible" thought, the product of Mind, can influence and change physical matter, a theory that Soviet experimenters in parapsychology are reported to be carrying out in fact. They've taken apart the old belief that we must use tools to create engines that apply *physical* force to accomplish these things and are proceeding under the assumption that the ancient sages were onto something when they repeatedly stated it could be done *directly* by the power of thought itself.

Ten years ago such a statement would have been greeted with scorn and derision on just about any campus of any college or university in America. But at this particular juncture in history, Homo sapiens is undergoing a fantastically far-reaching psychic revolution. Only a tiny fraction of this activity has surfaced in the mass media—and not *all* of it is valid. But if we, at what seems to be our present relatively primitive state of evolution, are awakening to the reality of astrology and other similar intangibles, it's hard to keep from wondering about *other* species of beings in far-flung parts of the Galaxy.

Nearly everyone is familiar with the odds, the law of averages, or the "chances" of life existing on other worlds. Intelligent beings that may be anywhere from a century to a hundred million years ahead of us in science, knowledge, wisdom, in strange, alien transcendant states of consciousness and dimensions so far beyond what we think of as wisdom that the human intellect may be as incapable of such awareness as an amoeba is incapable of sensing the existence or nature of the biologist who studies it under his microscope.

Whether we accept the word of any individual researcher, all the evidence—the "accepted" evidence—at hand overwhelmingly points to the existence of vast, far-flung civilizations stretching across our Galaxy and throughout the infinite multitude of galaxies in our sphere of consciousness—and beyond.

It now appears that Energy Fields control living matter and that these fields are literally indestructible. Moreover, our Minds are synchronous with that which Dr. Penfield calls the "T-field." It should therefore follow that life on other worlds—perhaps entire *aggregates* of worlds—throughout the Universe conform to those L-fields which in turn mold the life forms to thrive amid physical conditions which the human body in its present form could neither endure nor survive.

Within this frame of reference, the T-fields of very advanced alien cultures might not only be able to effect their environment directly (as human experiments with PK—psychokinetic energy—indicate is possible), to create whatever environment happens to be desirable at any given time, but that (conversely) these energy fields might also be employed to change their physical forms in some super chameleon way in order to adapt to *any* environment at will. American and Soviet experiments with the genetic "code" are already being undertaken to prove the feasibility of creating test-tube babies born "in vitro" or altering future generations of artificially nurtured humanoids to live and breathe beneath the Earth's oceans like fish, to survive in the rarified atmosphere of Mars without protection, or to inhabit any hostile environment anywhere in the Galaxy.

In some manner we are not yet equipped to understand, part of the function of our brain is to act as a kind of extra-dimensional radio receiver/transmitter for the T-field, which has the well-known property of existing—as far as we know—eternally—a concept the physical brain cannot truly comprehend.

T-fields also appear to be the force that holds atoms as well as molecules together. They are the cohesive force that forms the mold of the physical world we live in. Related in some unfathomable way to gravity, they seem to be of the same order of energy that impels the planets in their orbits around the Sun and causes the Sun to burn its "nuclear" fires for billions and billions of years, apparently consuming its own mass over and over, yet never diminishing itself.

Pascal Jordan, the German physicist and Nobel Prize winner and Albert Einstein's former collaborator, Dr. Banesh Hoffmann, said in a joint statement that "A gravitational field seems to have some similarity with the force which transmits telepathic information, in that both act at a distance and penetrate all obstacles."

And the well-known Soviet parapsychologist, Professor Leonid L. Vasilier, professor of physiology at the University of

Leningrad, proved that mental communication and even long-distance hypnotic influencing occurs regularly, that it is not impeded either by obstacles or distance, that it has no connection with electromagnetic radiation, and *cannot be explained by physics!* Furthermore, as noted earlier, these T-fields can attach themselves to, or localize themselves in, any kind of matter of any shape or size!

The Fields of Life concentrate the same care and attention on the nervous and digestive systems, say, of a sand flea as to the brain of a whale or any of the uncountable number of life forms on this planet alone. The *Universal* T-field also interacts with inanimate matter as the cohesive, all-embracing force that holds atoms and molecules together and the mold that forms and shapes the stars and planets and decrees their velocity and juxtaposition to one another. Of course, the expansion of the Universe which astronomers interpret from the red shift in the spectra of distant stars and galaxies may indicate that universal gravity is very "slowly" (from our viewpoint) loosening its grip.

Even magnetic fields in the Earth's crust have preserved their intangible shapes for untold ages. Within the *detectable* electromagnetic spectrum, the pulses received from distant radio stars have preserved the *pattern* of their fields for thousands—even millions—of years, during which these fields have been flashing earthward at 186,792 miles per second (the speed of light). These same images are received sharply and clearly on the photo plates of the world's observatories. Some of the *more* distant galaxies may have since disintegrated or moved into some extradimensional plane beyond this Universe (as do dwarf stars which become "black holes" and disappear beyond all detection). But the *images* hold together and continue on—apparently forever.

The remarkable fact is that virtually the same image can be picked up from just about any other point in the Universe. In itself, that's a kind of miracle.

Despite everything materialistic science does to separate or eliminate the influence of the human Mind or T-field in its attempts to better understand the Universe, the downgrading of teleology (purposefulness) has reduced astronomy to an empty husk of dead, dry facts and measurements—with no life, no purpose, and no significance—as though it is one vast, dreary accident that we must somehow put up with. Think what this attitude makes of human existence!

The "now" physics and parapsychology are forcing more and more old-line astronomers to accept evidence for the existence of a nonphysical—or at least extraphysical—Reality. Because every scientific advance is made by a human Mind, a group of scientists from Columbia University recently announced that ESP or clairvoyant ability probably accounted for the success of many scientists, businessmen, and executives and was the key factor behind most great scientific breakthroughs. In other words, those who have the most readily accessible channel to their "superconscious" Mind (another term for the T-field) are most successful in life.

Since the advent of the first few generations of computers, man has relied increasingly on technology to extend his sensory range—both microscopically *and* cosmically—over his environment. This was frequently detrimental to the infinitely broader, more sensitive energy of Mind, paradoxically the force which is responsible for creating the very technology that causes Mind to be discounted.

The Mind or T-field that molds and energizes our physical bodies and brains is *always* in touch with the local gravitational field of the solar system *and* with the *Universal* L-field. Logically then, *Mind is never out of contact with any point in the Universe!*

The foregoing suggests that communication with nonhuman Beings—be they in the vicinity of Ursa Major or anywhere else in the Galaxy—has probably *always* been within human capability. It makes no difference whether the method is psionics, with a psychic boost from something like the Hieronymus Machine or Lawrence's biodynamic field receptor, or even directly—from *Mind to Mind.*

Rigid enforcement of the stringent scientific method as a kind of quasireligion—with its burdensome rote and tradition—may be the most serious obstacle in the way of direct communication between Genus Terran and any of the myriad civilizations that must be thriving all over the Universe—definitely in nearby galaxies, certainly within our own Galaxy, probably in nearby star systems, and possibly within our own solar system.

Through a concerted and serious study of these new fields of knowledge, mankind may take the first step toward direct interspecies contact—the greatest adventure in human history.

Chapter Twelve

The End
of the Beginning

"One measures a circle," Charles Fort said, "beginning anywhere." Fort's universe consisted of an infinite number of forms, none of which were distinguishable from the others. A cloud or a stone, a microbe or a tree, a man or a star—one thing blended into and influenced the other.

The only way this could be true would be if there was nothing but energy in the Universe—energy manifesting in an infinite number of ways. This is the Universe of psionics, the field that encompasses radionics and radiesthesia, i.e., (respectively) the analysis and treatment of plant and insect life and the diagnosis and treatment of human beings.

Something strange has happened, and continues to happen, in the field of psionics. Why, for example, have there been no new applications for radionic device patents since the late 1950s? According to Jacob Rabinow, associate director of the U.S. Office of Invention and Innovation, "Americans have simply stopped inventing. As a result, the United States has dropped to seventh place in world patenting of new ideas."

Curtis P. Upton, William J. Knuth, and Howard H. Armstrong got together with Brigadier General Henry Gross in the late 1940s and formed U.K.A.C.O. corporation. The treatments made by the machines these learned and humanitarian scientists and engineers invented and used were originally called "electronic," "radiotonic," "biotonic," and even "homeotronic." Their contracts with farmers were concluded only when radionic control of insects fully satisfied the agriculturists. Naturally, any system as successful and inexpensive as theirs claimed to be *should* have met with widespread success.

186

While growing numbers of enthusiastic farmers spread the story of the amazing U.K.A.C.O. treatment, the chemical and fertilizer industries girded for battle. Psionics was then (and continues to be) very bad news for them. A campaign of vilification, enthusiastically supported by scientists, was begun.

General Gross, in an interview with the author, issued a simple description of the U.K.A.C.O. process:

"The purpose of the process is to stimulate vegetation of all kinds and to kill or drive away insect pests from this vegetation. The process is electronic and the action is accomplished by the use of a small radio-like box almost like an audio or radio amplification mechanism modified at the input and the broadcast ends. The set or box is composed of a copper collector plate plugged into the input of the machine which may be activated either by the 110-volt system or, as we have recently found, several stages of transistors replacing radio tubes and using dry cell batteries. Types of impulses are picked up on the plate, carried through condensers and tubes, or transistors, and broadcast from a small antenna attached to the box. The machine is grounded and may be operated in the open air or within doors.

"Strange as it sounds, we have, for four years, been doing the following: If it is desired to stimulate a tree or a plant, a leaf of that tree or plant may be taken and placed upon the collector plate of the machine. The current is turned on for approximately five or ten minutes and some pattern from the leaf is broadcast in all directions, but is only effective in and received by the parent tree or plant from which the leaf came, with resultant stimulation darkening of the green color in the tree, increasing the length of new growth in the spring. In the case of a quick growing plant the increase in size and vitality is visible within a period of weeks; with the tree, treatments in one season show in the new growth in the spring as well as particularly.

"If a tree or plant is infected with aphids, for instance, the leaf is put on the collector plate and also a small amount of a suitable reagent which has been found by trial to be obnoxious to the insect. Upon the operation of the machine, elec-

tronic qualities of the reagent are carried with those same waves of the leaf to the source growth and the insects are killed or leave the vegetation, usually within 48 hours. This may be operated at a distance of several miles from the object being treated.

"When it is desired to treat, for instance, a corn field infested with Japanese beetles, we have found that instead of a leaf of a single plant we can treat an entire field by using the original photographic film of an aerial photograph, using only that portion which applies to the field in question. For processes of control, we usually cut a corner or a strip off the picture of the field so that by inspection the degree of elimination of insects may be observed on the ground.

"Using a small amount of a suitable reagent (rotenone, etc.) placed on the collector plate with the photographic film (dull side down), and operating the machine for from five to ten minutes, several treatments usually suffice to kill or drive away beetles from the treated area up to 80 or 90% elimination while they remain 100% in the untreated or controlled portion.

"The Pennsylvania Farm Bureau put their Research Department on an investigation of this process and after a year of tests and observation and the accomplishing of the same effects by operating machines themselves, made a contract with us for the exclusive use of the process in Pennsylvania. The verification of a great number of test treatments is available in the Pennsylvania Farm Bureau and may be thoroughly examined and checked."

More than 90 farms in the Cumberland Valley were successfully treated with U.K.A.C.O. psionic machines. Then word spread to the West coast, and farmers whose problems outweighed their incredulity became supporters and defenders of the burgeoning science of radionics.

Here are a few of the scores of letters General Gross received:

CORTARO MANAGEMENT COMPANY
229 W. Alameda St.
Tucson, Ariz.

Mr. R. S. McCandliss
Monterey County Farm Bureau
126 Lincoln Avenue
Salinas, California

Dear Mr. McCandliss:

We have been using UKACO radionic control of an experimental 80 acres in the middle of some 480 acres of Acala X-44 short staple cotton. Other growers in the area, notably Louis Anway and Earl Horton, who between them operate very extensive holdings, have used the process at the same time.

Our experience, and frankly we are somewhat mystified, has been that on our 80 and on the 160 acre test plot of Mr. Anway, we found no occasion to use any insecticides. On the adjacent fields, however, our costs for insecticides, applied both by tractor and by airplane, were in excess of $8.00 an acre.* Mr. Anway's experience was the same. Everybody and his brother checked the test field for bugs.

Our experience was that there would be a light infestation of harmful insects and we suffer, of course, from the ligus, the corn ear worm and the like, but the insects would appear and disappear without harmful results as the treatment progressed.

On our adjacent lands and on the lands of many growers in the general area, a rather serious infestation of aphis occurred. This was serious enough for the County agent to call a special meeting on the subject and some 60 growers and their representatives arrived. They found aphis all over the place, but not on the test plots.

Our position in this matter is that while we have made no scientific investigation, the practical results of this test lead us to the conclusion that as the Cortaro Management Co., we will use the process next year on our entire 2800 acres of cotton.

Frankly, we expect to have ulcers counting the bugs

*Author's note: this would be more than $26 an acre today.

189

next year, but if we get the same results on the whole project as we got on the test field we are going to save around $20,000 and we are willing to go to considerable effort for that substantial sum.

Please understand that this is neither a recommendation or a promotion. Our results could have been an accident; however, the representative of UKACO set out to do a certain thing and did it. We feel strongly that maybe this process gives promise of taking one good long advance in our eternal fight with insects.

We have not yet picked the cotton. It looks good. It seems to have approximately 20% more seed and this possibly may be the result of not destroying the bees, upon which the radionic process seems to have no effect.* It will be at least the middle of December before we complete the pick. Sampling tests and good judgment lead us to the fond hope that we are going to get around 1100 pounds to the acre. Let us pray.

Sincerely yours,
CORTARO MANAGEMENT CO.
W. S. Nicholas, Pres.

WSN/GE

It could have been the prayer; their yield averaged better than 1300 pounds per acre. Another grower and successful recipient of psionic treatment wrote:

To Whom It May Concern:
In reference to the control of insects in this area by the use of electronics. There has been several examples which I believe proves its effectiveness.

"I am farming 400 acres which is under electronics control and have had no insects in this field. My neighbor just across the road which is not under electronics has had to dust already.

"There are about 14,000 acres under cultivation in

---

*Author's note: Mr. Nicholas was unaware of the completely selective nature of psionic treatment.

this valley of which about 6,000 are under electronics control. None of the electronics controlled land has been dusted but most of the other land has already been dusted.

"Personally, I think electronics is very effective."

Edward Anway
Box 76
Marana, Arizona

Scientists and other agricultural bureaucrats of course, knew better. They didn't have to look to "know" that radionics was utter nonsense, as one stalwart put it, " . . . on the face of it."

Some scientists.

* * *

Here's a letter to one of Geu. Gross' radionic operators:

Marana Arizona
June 9, 1951

Dear Mr. Nash,
This is a statement as to what has occurred here with leaf worm in the last 48 hours.

We noticed a very heavy infestation of leaf worms the day before yesterday and yesterday. Today, for no apparent reason except for your treatment with electronics, the worms have disappeared and after a very close inspection, we could find no worms.

This is not a recommendation but merely a statement as to what I have seen with my own eyes.

(signed) *Harm Stubbe*
Rte. No. 1
Box 412
Tucson, Ariz.

The files of the Homeotronic Research Foundation in Pennsylvania contain the most valuable records of Curtis Upton's experiments—exact specifications of his instruments, details of the most useful and effective "reagents," records of his successes and failures, and notes on radionic techniques that should be avoided. General Gross, Curtis Upton, and their associates operated successfully in several states. First, they had aerial photographs taken, then diagnosed the needs of the farmers' land. In order to be sure that the radionics devices were never used for destructive (to human life) purposes, the two U.K.A.C.O. "boxes" were never sold to an outsider. The corporation maintained rigid control of their devices and trained others to use them properly.

They would install one of the instruments (they came in two sizes, one about the size of a portable sewing machine, the other just a couple times the size of a shoe box) in a farmhouse and plug into an electrical outlet. The "key" (a photograph, a leaf or some sap or juice from a tree) would be placed on the collector plate and the farmer told to switch the device on for about 10 or 15 minutes a day. When there was no power available, they'd use battery-operated, transistorized equipment. Later, as the indefatigably curious John W. Campbell discovered, the device could be operated completely *without* electrical power.

By some extraordinary stroke of illumination or inductive reasoning, Curtis Upton made the astounding discovery that a mere pencil mark on a piece of paper was every bit as effective a "key" as a leaf, some juice, a photograph, or—in the case of a human being—a spot of blood, a nail cutting, a lock of hair, or skin scraping. But the mark had to be specially made, according to a ritual Upton got from God only knows where. He'd ask the patient or person to be treated to sign his name or make some mark with a pencil that had been sharpened at *both* ends. (The pencil had previously been exposed to the field of a strong bar magnet in order to "erase the accumulated radiations of others.") The subject's thumb however, had to be touching the other end of the pencil as he signed the paper. Then Upton would put on a pair of rubber gloves, put the scrap of paper on the collector plate of his device, and make the diagnosis.

He did this with dozens of personal friends, most of whom corroborated the radionic analysis with regular medical diagnoses. In fact, some illnesses were detected radionically that went undiscovered by ordinary medical scrutiny and analyses.

Curtis Upton also used a graphite or "lead" pencil *key* made from a shrub or tree. With rubber gloves, he would hold one point of a pencil under the cambium layer and rub a piece of paper against the other point. Then the paper could be used in all subsequent treatments of the tree.

It sounds crazy as hell; in fact it is the utter simplicity of the process that causes the minds of the academically trained and oriented to boggle. The fact however is that psionics produces practical results, often witnesses and certified by intelligent men and women who are more interested in getting things done than in demanding immediate theoretical explanations of *how* a thing works. This shouldn't be construed as denigrating healthy scientific curiosity, but when a discovery is rejected or suppressed because there's no *theory* to explain its function, that's putting the cart before the horse.

Curtis Upton once invited B. A. Rockwell, then director of Research of the Pennsylvania Farm Bureau Cooperative Association, to witness his experiments and to check the results. Here's part of Rockwell's completely independent and unbiased response:

"Last August, I observed a most unusual experiment in insect control. By means of radionics, Mr. H. H. Armstrong . . . killed Japanese beetles from a distance of thirty-two miles! From the evidence at hand, might we assume that by means of radionic processes Jap beetles, potato and corn aphids and perhaps many other insect pests which injure farm and truck crops, orchards, woodlots, or ornamental trees and shrubs, can be controlled from a central location, over an area of thirty to forty miles in diameter and perhaps at even greater distances. Furthermore, the expense for such treatment would be so small to be almost unbelievable . . .

"All normal life on this Earth is a result of electro-chemical balance. When these two factors are in balance, the plant or the animal is strong and vigorous, resists disease and makes the most of its environment. When there is an electro-chemical unbalance, then retarded growth and disease take over.

"Until recently however, the writer has never witnessed anything that seemed to positively prove this electro-chemical theory. Last summer the writer personally examined rhubarb, peonies and fruit trees which had been broadcast with their own respective voltage vibrations amplified.

"The rhubarb and peonies were much larger and more vigorous than adjacent untreated plants, while the fruit trees' terminal growth was far in excess of its neighbors in the same environment. It appeared that these radionically treated plants were benefited ...

"Would it be erroneous to conclude that they were purged of poisons, harmonized and brought into electro-chemical balance? If it is possible to benefact plants by radionics then *why not animals, including humans?*"

Rockwell concluded: " ... the Pennsylvania Farm Bureau Co-operative Association believes there is enough positive evidence available to justify quite a comprehensive experimental program ... to further determine the possibilities of insect control by radionic processes."

Human beings, insects, plants, birds, fish, and microbes all share the animating, controlling L-field—an "aura" of energy that Mind alone is capable of affecting. These are the conditions of and for life on Earth—and very likely on other planets of other star systems of other galaxies throughout the Universe.

Psionics. The super science of the future. Once this is recognized and universally accepted, human destiny will truly be in the hands of Genus Terran. It is through these "refined energies" that we will most likely learn to establish contact and interstellar commerce with other intelligent beings somewhere out there.

Psionics may, in fact, be the key to the destiny of our species.

The overwhelming weight of the evidence convinces me that this is so.

Bibliography

Bell, A.H. (Editor). *Practical Dowsing*. London: G. Bell & Sons, 1965.

Burr, Harold Saxton. *Blueprint for Immortality*. London: Neville Spearman, 1972.

Davis, Albert Roy and Bhattacharya, A.K. *Magnets and Magnetic Fields*. Calcutta: Firma K. L. Mukhopadhayay Publishers, 1970.

Ferro and Grumley, Michael. *Atlantis: The Autobiography of a Search*. New York: Dell, 1970.

Goodavage, Joseph. *The Comet Kohoutek*. New York: Pinnacle Press, 1974.

Jung, C.J. and Pauli, W. *The Interpretation of Nature and the Psyche*. New York: Pantheon Books, 1955.

Koestler, Arthur. *The Roots of Coincidence*. New York: Random House, 1972.

Lethbridge, C. *The Monkey's Tail*. London: Routledge & Kegan Paul, 1969.

Lewinsohn, Richard. *Science, Prophecy and Prediction*. New York: Dell, 1961.

Long, Max Freedom. *The Secret Science at Work*. Los Angeles: DeVorss, 1953.

Luria, Salvatore. *Life: The Unfinished Experiment*. New York: Charles Scribner's Sons, 1973.

Maltz, Maxwell. *Psycho-Cybernetics*. Englewood Cliffs, New Jersey: Prentice-Hall, 1960.

Murchie, Guy. *Music of the Spheres*. New York: Dover Books, 1967.

Puharich, Andrija. *Beyond Telepathy*. Darton, Longoman & Todd, 1962.

Russell, Edward W. *Design for Destiny*. London: Neville Spearman, 1971.

Streeter, E. W. *Great Diamonds of the World*. New York: Gordon Press, 1882.

Toffler, Alvin. *Future Shock*. New York: Random House, 1970.

Troward, Thomas. *The Edinburgh Lectures on Mental Science*. New York: Dodd, Mead, 1909.

Troward, Thomas. *The Hidden Power*. New York: Dodd, Mead, 1921.

About the Author

Joseph Goodavage has written and published dozens of articles, both for scientific and general audience publications. Formerly science reporter and writer for the *New York Daily News* syndicate, the *Chicago Tribune* and *The New York Times,* Mr. Goodavage is a member of The American Society of Journalists and Authors, the New York Newspaper Guild, The American Federation of Astrologers, and the Authors Guild.

Mr. Goodavage's books for NAL include ASTROLOGY: THE SPACE AGE SCIENCE and WRITE YOUR OWN HOROSCOPE.

Other SIGNET and MENTOR Mystics
You'll Want to Read

☐ **THE COMPLETE ILLUSTRATED BOOK OF DIVINATION AND PROPHECY by Walter B. Gibson & Litzka R. Gibson.** Tarot cards, i ching, hand of fate, palmistry, playing-card forecasting, and many other methods of phophesying your future have been gathered in one volume, together with explanatory charts and diagrams and a glossary of divination, to make foretelling the future easier. (#E6525—$2.25)

☐ **THE AMAZING URI GELLER edited by Martin Ebon.** Is Uri Geller a psychic, the instrument of an alien intelligence seeking peaceful contact with Earth, or an adept fraud out to make his fame and fortune at the public's expense? Now, at last, the real story about the psychic of the century. With eight pages of astonishing photos. (#W6475—$1.50)

☐ **THE SUPERNATURAL by Douglas Hill and Pat Williams.** Two knowledgeable authorities, both of them journalists, lead an excursion into the realms of the unknown, presenting astonishing facts about witches and vampires, ghosts and poltergeists, grotesque cults and orgiastic rituals. (#W6174—$1.50)

☐ **PASSPORT TO THE SUPERNATURAL by Bernhardt J. Hurwood.** Travel through time and space to the most frightening limits of your imagination with these fascinating tales of the occult and the supernatural from around the globe. (#ME1281—$1.75)

☐ **MANY MANSIONS by Gina Cerminara.** The most convincing proof of reincarnation and ESP ever gathered in one volume. A trained psychologist's examination of the files and case histories of Edgar Cayce, the greatest psychic of our time. (#W6811—$1.50)